Digital Ethnography

Digital Ethnography

Anthropology, Narrative, and New Media

BY NATALIE M. UNDERBERG AND ELAYNE ZORN

University of Texas Press ⬥ *Austin*

Requests for permission to reproduce material from this work should be
sent to:
    Permissions
    University of Texas Press
    P.O. Box 7819
    Austin, TX 78713-7819
    utpress.utexas.edu/index.php/rp-form

♾ The paper used in this book meets the minimum requirements of
ANSI/NISO Z39.48-1992 (R1997) (Permanence of Paper).

Library of Congress Cataloging-in-Publication Data to come
Underberg, Natalie M.
Digital ethnography : anthropology, narrative, and new media /
by Natalie M. Underberg and Elayne Zorn. — 1st ed.
        p.   cm.
Includes bibliographical references and index.
ISBN 978-0-292-76025-3
1. Anthropology—Computer network resources.   2. Digital media.
3. Digital communications.   4. Communication in anthropology.
5. Digital video.   6. Video recording in ethnology.   I. Zorn, Elayne.
II. Title.
GN13.5.U63   2013
301.0285—dc23   2012029243

doi:10.7560/744332

First paperback edition, 2014

To Elayne Zorn
Colleague, mentor, friend

Contents

Acknowledgments **ix**

Introduction **1**

1. Rethinking Culture through Multimedia Ethnography **17**

2. Florida and Peru: Experiments in Ethnographic Representation **28**

3. Digital Tools for Anthropological Analysis **42**

4. Using the Extensible Markup Language in Cultural Analysis and Presentation **48**
   NATALIE UNDERBERG AND RUDY MCDANIEL

5. Using Features of Digital Environments to Enable Cultural Learning **66**

6. Cultural Heritage Video Game Design **74**

Conclusion. Narratives and Critical Anthropology: Roles for New Media **82**

Appendix: Guide to Web-Based Materials   **91**

Glossary   **93**

References Cited   **99**

Index   **III**

Acknowledgments

As I write this, my coauthor, the late Elayne Zorn, is not here to add her acknowledgments. She is still with us: in this book, in the PeruDigital project, and in our hearts.

This book would not have been possible without the support and collaboration of many parties, including family, friends, and colleagues. The projects on which this book is based have received financial and programmatic support from a number of organizations, both internal and external to the University of Central Florida (UCF). At UCF, the School of Visual Arts and Design (formerly Digital Media); the Latin American, Caribbean, and Latino Studies Program; the Center for Humanities and Digital Research; CREATE (Center for Research and Education in Arts, Technology and Entertainment); the Office of International Studies; the College of Arts and Humanities; and the UCF In-House Research Grant Program have all provided funding for one or more of the projects included in this book. External funding has been received from the Florida Humanities Council and the National Endowment for the Humanities (for the "Andean World" Summer Institute). In addition, the Pontifical Catholic University of Peru–Lima, in particular the Institute of Ethnomusicology, has been a valued collaborator in this research.

This project would not have been possible without the emotional support of my family, friends, and colleagues. I have my parents to thank for always encouraging me to follow my passions, and my friends both at and outside of UCF for their words of encouragement. In addition, I have been extremely fortunate to receive the support and wise advice of a number of faculty and administrators at UCF, in particular, José Fernández, Terry Frederick, Leslie Lieberman, José Maunez-Cuadra, Stella Sung, and David Vickers.

My field is an inherently collaborative endeavor, requiring that people from many different areas of expertise work together toward a common goal. I have had the pleasure and honor of working with a number of very talented colleagues over the years. In particular, I would like to thank Kristin Congdon, director of the UCF Cultural Heritage Alliance, for all of her wisdom and for her dedication to the field of Florida folk art and its documentation. I am also immensely grateful for the contributions of the late Chantale Fontaine to the success of the alliance during the years I served as project coordinator. In addition, I have been fortunate to have had the opportunity to work with my fellow digital media colleague Rudy McDaniel over the years on several projects and hope we can continue to collaborate in the future.

To my colleagues and students in the UCF Digital Ethnography Lab, my sincere gratitude. The PeruDigital project has benefited from the expertise and skills of many people, first among them of course my coauthor, Elayne Zorn, the late project codirector. In addition, admiration and thanks go to the faculty and student team who worked with us in building and refining the pilot project, in particular Jo Anne Adams, Melissa Cafcules, Beth Hallmann, Si-Jung "Jun" Kim, Norma Ledesma, Susana Molina, Omar Vera Muniz, and Ed Porch.

Finally, having had the pleasure and honor of being Elayne Zorn's friend and colleague for several wonderful years, I would like to thank her mother, Sandra Gordon, and her son, Gavriel Cutipa-Zorn, for their unfailing encouragement and support.

Natalie M. Underberg
Orlando, Florida

Introduction

You open your eyes and take a look around the Plaza Francia in an old section of downtown Lima, Peru. Pivoting, you see a cerulean church with an elaborate rose window. Opposite this ecclesiastical structure you spot a man wearing an intricately woven vest that falls just below his mid-chest. He's standing next to a light green kiosk around which various books, flyers, and newspapers are stored. Intrigued, you walk up to him and he greets you:

> Good day! I moved to Lima a while back but have fond memories of my home, Puno. Take a look at some of the materials in the kiosk to learn about the city of Puno and its many types of music and festivals. Our Virgin of Candelaria festival is renowned throughout the Americas!

Encouraged by such a friendly greeting, you pick up a copy of the kiosk newspaper *La Semanal de Puno* (*The Puno Weekly*), which announces the procession of the Mamita Candelaria. The headline is juxtaposed with a magnificent photo of the Virgin of Candlemas carried aloft on an elaborate pink float.

This initial encounter has whetted your curiosity. Walking away from the kiosk toward the other end of the Plaza Francia, you encounter a young woman sitting on one of the plaza's benches, holding a guitar. Under the shade of a palm tree, her hair lightly tossed by the breeze, she seems just a little sad, or

Introductory scene for PeruDigital interactive environment. Courtesy: Natalie M. Underberg.

maybe pensive. You think, maybe if I talk to her she'll tell me something about herself.

You're rewarded with this personal reflection: "Hello! I'm far from my hometown in northern Peru, but when I look at my guitar I remember my Morropón." She then tells you that a recording of her singing a *tondero*—a Spanish-derived musical and dance style that incorporates African percussion unique to her hometown—can be found in Peru's renowned Institute of Ethnomusicology, the offices of which, she thinks, are just on the other end of the plaza.

You are intrigued and decide to visit the institute's archive and see what you can learn about the experiences of the people you've just met. You see a police officer standing on the corner and ask him if he knows how to get to the archive; he gives you directions and encourages you to visit.

You make the quick trip to the ethnomusicology archives—and you encounter a gold mine of information. Searching first the contents of the desk in the ethnographer's office, you find a calendar with festival dates recorded on it. You look for paper on which to record this information and find a yellow spiral-bound notebook on the desk. Forgetting for the moment the initial reason you were looking for paper, you find yourself delving into what looks like ethnographic fieldwork notes on a variety of topics, including the *tondero* the young woman told you about. Looking behind you, you realize there's a screen hanging on the wall. Searching for the projector, you find it, push "play," and are amazed to see the very same woman from the plaza singing about her beloved hometown—and the lyrics are not without a certain biting humor.

She sings: "Ya que quiero regresarme no tengo quién me transporte . . . Yo quiero muerto mi cholo y no mi pobre burrito" [I want to go back home but I don't have anyone to take me . . . I wish my man would have died instead of my poor burro]. How can a song be funny and sad at the same time? What's so wonderful about her hometown that makes her nostalgic for it?

Turning to the right, you find a bookshelf filled with books. One is about the region of Piura, where she says she's from. Maybe you can start there. You think: There's so much to learn, and to do this I have to learn to ask the right questions of the

Virtual ethnographer's office in the PeruDigital interactive environment. Courtesy: Natalie M. Underberg.

people I meet, take notes on what I've learned, and consult the writings and recordings about the topics about which I'm curious. Got it. I'm playing the role of an ethnographer, virtually, in the PeruDigital website.

The Role of the Anthropologist in the New Media Landscape

Anthropologists have become increasingly concerned with the intersection between culture and technology in the twenty-first century. As the authors of this book, we were drawn to this emerging field based on our perspectives as anthropologists, folklorists, and ethnographers. Underberg develops and studies the use of digital media projects to preserve and represent folklore and cultural heritage, specializing in the literary side of cultural anthropology and the cultural studies side of literary theory. She uses her training to conceive of, design, manage, and study the production of digital media projects that deal with culture and folklore. Zorn was a cultural anthropologist interested in how indigenous peoples in the Andes cope with globalization, particularly in the area of traditional arts. Underberg and Zorn founded the Digital Ethnography Lab at the University of Central Florida (UCF) in Orlando, Florida, to work with other scholars and members of the communities they research to examine the process of digital adaptation of cultural materials and to investigate the social impact of new technologies, with the goal of responsibly integrating technology into cultural representations. This research reaches across several areas related to the nexus of digital media and anthropology covered in this book: digital media as a tool for creative expression, anthropological research, and heritage-based education.

In this book, we focus on digital media in relation to cultural anthropology. Several projects have been developed—and new ones are being created at a rapid pace—that incorporate the use of new technologies into anthropology's other subfields: archaeology, physical (biological) anthropology, and linguistic anthro-

UCF Digital Ethnography Lab website. Courtesy: Natalie M. Underberg.

pology. In addition, a growing number of projects present cultural heritage materials, such as the ChinaVine project (www .chinavine.org). Digitization projects make collections of objects, texts, and audio and visual recordings available to the world—or more properly, that part of the world with Internet access. Those without access, primarily in the Global South, face a serious problem that scholars need to address.

Anthropologists from all subfields collaborated to develop the widely praised RACE: Are We So Different? (www.under standingrace.org/HOME.HTML). This website incorporates interviews, games, quizzes, and a variety of other approaches to reframe the discussion about race.

In anthropology, archaeologists (whose projects require specialists from many disciplines) are collaborating with colleagues to map and model ancient sites using digital technologies. The use of new technologies to assist traditional methods for mapping can result in the rapid identification of new features, as was the case at the Maya site of Caracol, Belize, where overflights using LIDAR (light detection and ranging) produced impressive results (Chase, Chase, and Weishampel 2010).

Biological anthropologists worked with computer scientists to scan the famous hominid fossil known as Lucy with a high-resolution CT to create a "virtual Lucy" to study (Solomon

2009). The Becoming Human website uses interactive media, including an interactive timeline, to help users learn about human evolution (www.becominghuman.org/).

Linguistic anthropologists, increasingly working with source communities, are rushing to document oral literatures and local languages along with other materials collected in fieldwork sites. For example, the Digital Himalaya project website presents materials collected in the Himalayan region such as older ethnographic films, journals, map collections, rare books (in PDF format), archives of different forms of data about little-known ethnic groups (e.g., the Thangmi), and other materials (www .digitalhimalaya.com).

As noted, digitization of museum and archival collections preserves fragile materials and expands access to them. One example of many such digitization projects is being carried out at the Institute of Ethnomusicology at the Pontifical Catholic University of Peru–Lima. The institute, with support from a number of donors (such projects are extremely expensive), is digitizing all its audiovisual holdings to secure their preservation and increase access to its collections. Many other digitization projects can be found online, such as the Billie Jean Isbell Andean Collection: Images from the Andes; this site, created with support from the Cornell University Library, presents approximately 1,500 photographs taken during more than three decades of research, as well as song texts and publications, and also seeks to preserve this data and expand access to these materials beyond the ethnographer's office (isbellandes.library.cornell.edu/). Many more examples could be given.

Anthropology, Digital Media, and Culture

As we discuss in this book, anthropologists were relatively slow to adopt the use of computers as well as to consider the effects of digital technology generally on their field (though as these websites and this book demonstrate, this is changing). Traditionally, most anthropologists do not receive computer science training in current anthropology curricula, at least in the United States. Yet, anthropologists themselves may be the best prepared to understand the impact of digital media on culture and to use their expertise in ethnographic methods to influence the use and even design of new technologies (see, for example, cultural anthropologists Neil Whitehead and Michael Wesch's [2009] recent article in *Anthropology News* for a thoughtful discussion of digital media's impact on the wider field of anthropology). Digital technology is expanding at an exponential rate. With increased collaboration between technical experts and cultural experts, we have the opportunity—no, the obligation—to see that this technology is used in culturally responsible and responsive ways.

In the early days of the developing collaboration between computer science and anthropology, the main question was, How much computer science do anthropologists need to know? A related question has arisen with the increased ubiquity and "user-friendliness" of digital technology (such as video-editing software programs like iMovie and instant web page templates like blogs and wikis): How much technology does the public (or, in older anthropological parlance, do informants) need to know to create their own self-representations? The popularity of digital storytelling, for example (see the website of the Center for Digital Storytelling: www.storycenter.org), has advanced the idea that ordinary members of the public can learn the technology for self-expression sufficiently well to create their own films—with no need for the documentarian (or ethnographic filmmaker, for that matter). If, similarly, everyone can make her or his own website, what is the role of the ethnographer?

This question is still being explored, but we suggest that the anthropologist-as-translator (of culture but not as critic; see Asad 1986) is still essential in the new media environment, at least to enable certain visually and technologically sophisticated representations of culture. It takes someone years to learn how to use software such as Dreamweaver, Photoshop, and Flash, which are some of the principal programs used to build complex websites like Folkvine.org (www.folkvine.org) or PeruDigital (www .perudigital.org). Commensurate understanding of game design and programming is required to create a game mod such as the Turkey Maiden Educational Computer Game.

And it is not, as some digital media students believe, just the software that needs to be learned. Digital media study involves learning principles of visual design and interactivity, among others. Just as there are technological experts, so there are cultural experts—not only in the sense of understanding a culture but also in understanding how to understand a culture and how to communicate that information to nonmembers. Increasingly, we believe, this may be the role of the anthropologist in the new technological landscape: understanding and communicating between different groups to accomplish culturally responsible aims. We argue that this holds true whether the anthropologist is, as has historically been the case, from outside the culture or, increasingly, native anthropologists (people from the cultures they study) with particular insight into the culture.

Anthropologists, we argue, have an important role to play in new media design and development. Their commitment to understanding the impact of computer technology on culture compels much-needed attention to considerations of power, embodiment, and identity markers in digital culture. One particular area in which the expertise of anthropologists is needed concerns developing collaborative methodologies for digital media work. Forte (2004), for example, discusses engaging in online action research—a variant of action research in which ethnographers work with research partners on the creation of websites about their culture. Moore and Hennessey (2006), meanwhile, conduct research into how indigenous people use digital technologies for self-representation.

This work resonates well with the field of participatory design (PD) in human-computer interaction (HCI) studies, which involves potential users as well as multidisciplinary scholars working together. Ethnographers working on a digital media project would make an important contribution by transforming the research process through collaborative partnerships. Their expertise is needed, for example, in advising on how to carry out new media projects in a way that is consistent with traditional forms of social interaction and in building the so-called social infra-structure of such projects to ensure community participation.

In addition to advising on and managing relationships with community participants in the development of new media projects, anthropologists with additional training in digital media design and production (such as in the areas of transmedia story creation, digital media production, and game design) are necessary to ensure proper communication between ethnographers and cultural consultants on the one hand and research and technical production teams on the other. This would lead to increased communication and collaboration between scholars, technical experts, and community members. Just as ethnographers need to learn the culture of the community in which they live in order to function in it and convey this knowledge to an audience, so digital ethnographers need to learn the culture of digital media production and design in order to communicate and work successfully with technical experts and ensure that the new media work in which they participate reflects the voices and values of the cultures they study. For example, given the potential in humanities computing to design searchable databases that reflect categories and search models important to humanities scholars, anthropologists are able to engage in database design projects based on indigenous and other non-Western ways of thinking and organizing the world.

Another important role for anthropologists in the field of new media concerns using their expertise to advise on the creation of virtual representations of cultural experience, including the ethnographic encounter itself. In participatory design (PD) terms, this would refer to prototyping and evaluating the use of new media to represent cultures. Ethnographers working in multidisciplinary teams of scholars and technical experts can collaborate with artists and communities to conceive of an exploratory and experiential way to present cultural ideas and to identify how to integrate key cultural ideas into project design. As new media scholars know, new opportunities are emerging for a form of digital cultural representation that simulates cultural ideas, values, and experience, and anthropologists should be at the forefront of such work. In this way, anthropologists could serve an important function in such digital media projects by opening up the interpretive process and production experience.

Digital Ethnography

Digital ethnography, as we define it in this book, is a method for representing real-life cultures through combining the characteristic features of digital media with the elements of story. These projects use the expressive and procedural potential of computer-based storytelling to enable audiences to go beyond absorbing facts about another culture to entering into the experience of that culture. Through interactivity and immersion, we believe, digital media can enable anthropologists and folklorists to tell innovative cultural stories and re-create aspects of ethnographic methodology for a diverse audience. This book focuses on the methods of designing the layout and navigation of new media forms like websites and computer games to embed both cultural context and interpretation into the user experience.

This approach emerged out of an interest in employing new media as an expressive medium for ethnographic storytelling. Contemporary cultural anthropologists have come to understand their work to be as much a narrative as a scientific undertaking (Geertz 1988; Clifford and Marcus 1986; Van Maanen 1988). Digital ethnography involves adapting and transforming these ethnographic storytelling techniques across multiple forms of new media.

Beyond bringing together primary data with scholarly interpretation, this approach seeks to creatively exploit the immersive and interactive qualities of new media environments to simulate aspects of ethnographic methodology and cultural narratives. Such work takes a cue from the emerging subfield of multimedia ethnography and, in particular, multisensory multimedia ethnography. This work powerfully reminds us that ethnography is both process and product, and culture is as much about feelings and the senses as it is a matter of thinking and being (Marion and Offen 2009). For example, Sarah Pink's (2003) work is particularly instructive here. Writing about what she terms "sensory ethnography," Pink points to the potential of hypermedia to provide new forms of interlinking and configuring ethnographic video, film, and writing. Emerging media forms like hypermedia, she asserts, are as yet still finding their particular niche within ethnography (Pink 2003; see also Coover 2003).

In addition to visual, literary, and multimedia ethnography, digital ethnography takes a cue from hypertext theory and digital heritage work in the humanities and virtual heritage studies. For example, Murray's (1997) now classic discussion of the characteristics of digital environments in relation to storytelling offers ethnographers myriad ideas for developing innovative new media projects. According to Murray (1997), interactive and immersive digital environments are made possible by the following four properties of the computer as medium: the procedural (able to carry out a series of rules), participatory (interactive), spatial (representing a user-navigated space), and encyclopedic (capable of storing and retrieving large quantities of data). Ideas for how to exploit the characteristic features of new media for creative cultural expression will be discussed throughout the book. In particular, through projects like Nicario Jiménez's website on PeruDigital, we explore how ethnographic insights about ways of seeing and being in a culture can be conveyed using immersion, interaction, and the kinds of virtual embodiment new media enables.

Electronic culture, in general, reconfigures the behaviors and interrelationships of authors, audiences, and texts (Packer and Jordan 2002; Bolter 2001; Landow 2006; Murfin and Ray 1997; and Murray 1997). Bolter (2001), for example, outlines several defining characteristics of electronic text that distinguish it from the long history of print culture that preceded it. These include electronic text's capacity for flexibility, interactivity, creating multiple paths and voices, simulating a sense of space, and enabling readers to act like authors. In place of linear and single-author texts delivered in a static medium, digital media creates a spatially inflected nonlinear presentation that brings together disparate voices and empowers audiences to affect their encounters with texts.

The capacity of the computer to enable new forms of data analysis has inspired some anthropologists to develop new tools to facilitate the coding and contextualization of their fieldwork findings. The Cardiff University website Hypermedia Ethnography (www.cf.ac.uk/socsi/hyper/index.html), for example, offers information on three projects that use hypermedia in ethnographic research: the Production of Hypermedia Ethnography, Ethnography for the Digital Age, and Methodological Issues in Qualitative Data Sharing and Archiving. Using digital media to advance data analysis and manipulation aims, to be discussed in more detail in Chapter 3, allows anthropologists to produce richer ethnographic documents as well as potentially offering new ways to interpret the data itself. Digital anthropology projects, such as the excellent Digital Ethnography Project (www.csus.edu/anth/researchDigitalEthnographyProject.html), consist of digitized ethnographic data and the application of markup languages that enable processing, definition, and presentation of data. This is in addition to efforts to use hypertext to present anthropological scholarship itself, such as *iNtergraph: Journal of Dialogic Anthropology* (www.intergraph-journal.com/enhanced/welcome2.htm).

These features of electronic culture as they apply to digital ethnography will be explored throughout this book. For example, Underberg and Rudy McDaniel (coauthor of Chapter 4) have attempted to leverage the flexibility and manipulability of digital information in the design of several digital cultural heritage projects using a metadata classification system known as the extensible markup language (XML).

Digital ethnography, then, uses new media's defining characteristics to represent the narrative trend in contemporary cultural anthropology. Multilinearity, immersion, and imitation enable audiences to better understand cultural knowledge by means of virtual experience.

The digital ethnography approach to conveying cultural knowledge through digital media is also informed by recent work in digital cultural heritage studies. The spatial and immersive capacities of digital media (Packer and Jordan 2002; Murray 1997) enable the representation of a sense of place so often linked to cultural heritage and history (Glassberg 1996). Through interactivity and the juxtaposition of multiple voices, so-called dialogic spaces can be created to allow students and the public to engage in formal and informal cultural heritage education (Calandra and Lee 2005).

Such work, of course, takes a cue from the research of anthropologists and others who have examined the culture of the contemporary Internet and virtual worlds, such as Wesch's (2009) work on the culture of the contemporary Internet and other forms of digital culture (mediated cultures.net) and Boellstorff's (2008) work on the ethnography of Second Life. While an exhaustive review of the literature on cyberethnography is outside the scope of this book, mention should be made of a handful of the ethnographic studies of online cultures and online resources that have attended to the characteristic forms of representation and interaction in cyberspace, such as Hine (2000), Paccagnella (1997), Miller and Slater (2001), Cyber Anthropology (www.carle ton.ca/~bgiven/cyberant.htm), and the Cyber Anthropology Page (www.fiu.edu/~mizrachs/cyberanthropos.html). The work of these scholars and others reminds us to attend to the effects of computer technology on human culture and to consider the ways in which virtual spaces can have their own culture.

Miller and Slater (2000), for example, argue that ethnographers need to resist a placeless, culture-less notion of cyberspace, and instead focus their attention on the myriad ways new technologies are actually used by real people in diverse real-world communities. They focus on the dynamics by which Trinidadians have integrated—and adapted—the Internet into their lives and identities, but their insights are useful to ethnographers working in a variety of cultural contexts. This area of research is also informed by the work of media ethnographers such as S. Elizabeth Bird (2003), who conducted research with focus groups to determine how different ethnic groups would design a hypothetical television show about Native Americans, and Rhonda Fair (2000), who examined how the design of Native Americans' websites was affected by their perceptions of white beliefs about their ethnic group. Considerations of how real-world culture and identity can be embedded in virtual spaces will be further discussed throughout the book.

Outline of this Book

The book focuses on specific projects in order to review the literature in the field and suggest future directions. Chapters 1 and 2 consider the potential of digital media to represent anthropological research and interpretation creatively. Chapter 1, "Rethinking Culture through Multimedia Ethnography," discusses how such research combines insights from diverse traditions including visual anthropology (pioneered by such scholars as Heider 2006), an area of human-computer interaction studies known as participatory design (Schuler and Namioka 1993; Watkins 2007), and hypertext studies (Bolter 2001; Landow 2006; Murray 1997).

Chapter 2, "Florida and Peru: Experiments in Ethnographic Representation," explores the application of these principles to recent examples of website design. In its use of narrative principles, we see this area of work as a descendant of the tradition of literary ethnography, pioneered by such anthropologists as Oliver La Farge in *Laughing Boy: A Navajo Love Story* (2004 [1929]), Margaret Mead in *Coming of Age in Samoa* (1930), Laura Bohannan in *Return to Laughter: An Anthropological Novel* (1964; published under the pen name of Elenore Smith Bowen), and Zora Neale Hurston in *Their Eyes Were Watching God* (1998 [1937]). This tradition was later developed in such ethnographies as Barbara Myerhoff's *Number Our Days: A Triumph of Continuity and Culture among Jewish Old People in an Urban Ghetto* (1980), Karen McCarthy Brown's *Mama Lola: A Vodou Priestess in Brooklyn* (2001), and Ruth Behar's *Translated Woman: Crossing the Border with Esperanza's Story* (2003 [1993]), as well as in experimental ethnographies (what Kirin Narayan [1999] calls "faction") such as Billie Jean Isbell's *Finding Cholita* (2009).

The next two chapters examine the use of computer technology to aid anthropologists in gathering, storing, analyzing, and sharing data, as well as to present research and scholarship. Chapter 3, "Digital Tools for Anthropological Analysis," explores how new technology impacts data collection. As new media scholars point out, the so-called network culture enables the creation of a more dialogical, participatory approach to presenting and interpreting cultural heritage.

Chapter 4, "Using the Extensible Markup Language in Cultural Analysis and Presentation," explores the use of the extensible markup language (XML) in three culture-oriented projects developed at UCF. XML is important to such projects because it can allow for more relevant searches within a database. These searches can go beyond simple keyword searches (as readers would be familiar with from using, say, an online library catalog), to enable users to search for content based on the usage of the keyword in a particular context. This enables users (cultural experts or consultants, for example) to code the data according to more sophisticated research parameters. As many anthropologists and folklorists are not trained in computer science (a trend that began to change as of 2009, when the first graduate degree in digital anthropology was launched in the United Kingdom), collaboration with technical experts is necessary. This can be structured in several ways; at UCF, the digital media faculty themselves are a mixture of technical experts, artists, and humanities scholars, and their students learn essential skills in digital media as part of the curriculum. This enables student-driven projects and research project collaborations between different faculty. These projects, linked to cultural heritage preservation aims, are explored in Chapter 4, including joint work over the last few years by Underberg and Rudy McDaniel (McDaniel has a background in computer science and literature).

Chapters 5 and 6 explore the use of digital media as a tool for teaching about culture. Chapter 5, "Using Features of Digital Environments to Enable Cultural Learning," explores how the characteristics of digital environments can facilitate cultural learning. Taking a cue from the literature on cyberspace and virtual heritage work, the chapter considers how the spatial and interactive trend in digital heritage creates new possibilities for cultural representation and simulation.

Chapter 6, "Cultural Heritage Video Game Design," focuses on an educational computer game project designed to teach about cultural heritage. The Turkey Maiden Educational Computer Game mod introduces students to the history and culture of Depression-era Ybor City, Florida, known for its historic cigar industry and Latin immigrant population. As we discuss in this chapter, creating navigable virtual environments based on cultural and historical materials requires understanding how spatial storytelling operates in computer games and how the game space itself can be imbued with cultural meaning.

This book concludes with "Narratives and Critical Anthropology: Roles for New Media." With this final chapter we seek to bring together several strands that have been woven throughout the book and indicate possible directions for future work in the emerging field of digital ethnography.

Periodically throughout the book, the reader will see a parenthetical boldface letter (**A**, **B**, **C**, etc.); these letters are keyed to the web-based materials listed in the appendix. We encourage readers to toggle back and forth between the book and website to more fully explore the field of digital ethnography.

CHAPTER I

Rethinking Culture
through Multimedia Ethnography

Multimedia Ethnography

Multimedia ethnography, as a conceptual and creative descendant of literary and visual ethnography, clearly demonstrates the boundary crossing that increasingly characterizes academic practice. We see this in the pioneering visual anthropology of Gregory Bateson and Margaret Mead starting in the 1940s (Bateson and Mead 1942; also see Ruby 1996), as well as the interpretive work that encouraged literary anthropology, starting with Clifford Geertz in *The Interpretation of Cultures* [1973]; see also, among others, Clifford and Marcus 1986; Geertz 1988; Van Maanen 1988).

In our work, we have found that cultural experiences and ideas can be represented by digital media through digital culture projects. In this way we seek to re-create cultures online by combining collaborative methodologies with digital technologies. These projects involve using our narrative and new media skills to design creative interactive story experiences that transform facts and figures into a creative expression. If it is true that anthropologists are as much storytellers as scientists, and given the centrality of narratives in our lives (and the realization that facts are so often presented in narrative form), we are inspired—no, compelled—to work with artists and communities in ways that involve them in the creation of those narratives (**A**).

Multisensory ethnography, or ethnography that uses a diverse set of media such as video, photographs, or digital media to communicate multisensory experience and knowledge, was the subject of a recent issue of *Anthropology News* (Marion and Offen 2009) that featured the PeruDigital project, among a dozen other digital media projects (Zorn and Underberg 2009), including Bridget McDonnell's collaborative visual work with the Somali Lenses photographic exhibition and Susanne Kuehling's project on capturing scent through visual documentation in communicating Oceanic domestic experiences. Multimedia and multisensory ethnography, then, acknowledges that ethnography is both process and product, and that culture itself is about more than being or thinking; it is also a matter of feeling and sensory engagement (Marion and Offen 2009). Other evidence of the future of anthropological research as rooted in experiential digital media is the recent establishment of a new series from an academic press devoted to multisensory ethnography (noted on the Society for Visual Anthropology's website: societyforvisualanthropology .org/).

The emerging research agenda outlined in this section concerns the intersection of narrative, ethnography, and new media, which includes digital and networked information and communication technologies. This approach involves two related activities: engaging in ethnographic storytelling using digital media and employing collaborative methods of using new technology. Specifically, this research involves studying the process of adapting materials collected in one medium (such as ethnographic photographs, film, or a traditional folktale) into another (the Internet, a computer game) in order to present cultural information using the techniques of narrative, as well as considering the social impact of new technologies through investigating new ways to integrate technology into cultural representation.

In this work, anthropologists and new media scholars employ digital media to turn historical and cultural materials into "storied places" that can engage audiences through interactivity (where user choices affect the outcome of the narrative or experience in digital media), immersion (the re-creation of the sense

Screenshot from the UCF Digital Ethnography Lab's Puerto Ricans in Central Florida, 1940s–1980s: A History. Courtesy: Natalie M. Underberg.

of a three-dimensional space in a two-dimensional one), and multivocality (the inclusion of multiple voices or perspectives in a way that subverts the traditional hierarchy between a singular, powerful author and a passive audience or reader; see Packer and Jordan 2002; Bolter 2001). The goal is to develop interpretive approaches that use the distinctive features of the digital environment to reflect recent reflexive, narrative, and collaborative developments in folklore and anthropology.

When we began the projects under discussion in this section, we had just established the Digital Ethnography Lab at the University of Central Florida (UCF) as a partnership between anthropology and digital media faculty. Intended to allow artists, anthropologists, folklorists, and others to express new insights into culture, the lab has focused on three projects: PeruDigital, a website about Peruvian festivals; Puerto Ricans in Central Florida, 1940s–1980s: A History, an oral history and digital media project; and the Turkey Maiden Educational Computer Game, a game mod designed to teach about 1930s history and culture of Ybor City, Florida. On the basis of Underberg's earlier work at the UCF Cultural Heritage Alliance, where she

developed the East Mims Oral History Project (pegasus.cc.ucf
.edu/~cha/mims/welcometomims.html) and served as folklorist
and later project director for the Folkvine.org project, we had
reason to believe that what we had learned about the intersection
between culture and technology might be useful to an anthropological audience.

Digital Ethnographic Storytelling

Understanding the potential for digital ethnographic storytelling involves grappling with new media's ability to tell a story.
As we discussed in the introduction, digital ethnography takes a
creative cue from the tradition of literary ethnography—the attempt to convey the experience of learning and living in a culture
through literary and narrative techniques. Mitchell and Charmaz (1998) offer a useful overview of the techniques of literary
ethnography that anthropologists use in transforming facts into
narratives based on those facts. In their chapter "Telling Tales
and Writing Stories: Postmodernist Visions and Realist Images
in Ethnographic Writing," they explain that such techniques include "(a) pulling the reader into the story, (b) re-creating experiential moods within the writing, (c) adding elements of surprise, (d) reconstructing the experience through written images,
and (e) creating closure on the story while simultaneously recognizing it as part of an ongoing process" (Mitchell and Charmaz
1998:228–229).

   Using Mitchell's creative nonfiction work, based on fieldwork
with survivalists (people who believe seriously in the possibility
of, and prepare for, serious social disruption), Charmaz analyzes
the literary techniques used in relating ethnographic experience
in story form. Literary ethnographers draw readers into their
tales by establishing context and building anticipation about
what will come next. For example, Mitchell shows images of a
white supremacist magazine, piquing readers' interest by noting
that it arrived at just the right moment—which raises the question, why? (Mitchell and Charmaz 1998).

Other techniques for effective ethnographic storytelling include re-creating experiential moods, adding elements of surprise, and reconstructing the experience through description. Mitchell and Charmaz suggest considering how an event or experience reflects a particular mood and then integrating this impression into the description. Charmaz points out that Mitchell combines such elements as interview quotes, an account of his own internal monologue, and reflections on the scene as it is unfolding. By shifting the mood as the story develops, they point out, suspense is created and the reader is better able to identify with the situation and the ethnographer's point of view. As Charmaz explains, Mitchell places the reader in the scene with him, allowing the reader to imagine adopting the role of the ethnographer and the interviewee (Mitchell and Charmaz 1998).

Mitchell and Charmaz also point out that part of the objective is to "distill the experience," meaning that the storyteller must selectively choose which interview excerpts and images to include and how to frame them. Mitchell, they note, provides the shape and form of the story, providing readers with enough distilled content to evoke the experience and elucidate the authors' interpretations (Mitchell and Charmaz 1998).

Finally, ethnographic storytelling involves creating closure on the story while simultaneously recognizing it as part of an ongoing process. Charmaz observes that Mitchell offers readers a simultaneously intriguing yet haunting ending. While the piece as a whole holds together well, the ending suggests that the drama will continue to unfold (Mitchell and Charmaz 1998).

Translating such insights into new media development involves attempting to "show rather than tell" events as they unfold and seeking to give the audience a taste of the overall experience rather than just presenting factual details. Hypermedia's interactive and nonlinear characteristics lend themselves well to conveying cultural information. Packer and Jordan (2002) outline five defining features of multimedia: integration (combining artistic forms and technology into hybrid expressive forms), interactivity (users' ability to directly manipulate and communicate through the media experience), hypermedia (linking media elements together to create an associative trail), immersion (the simulation of a three-dimensional environment), and narrativity (the use of the above features to create nonlinear story and media). These features structure the design logic and navigation experience of digital ethnographic storytelling.

Underberg (2006a, 2006b) has written on the creative use of digital media to enact ethnographic storytelling in the East Mims Oral History Project website. The project, funded by a UCF research grant on which Underberg was project director, told the story of East Mims, Florida, a historically African American community on the east coast of Central Florida. The project combined oral history and archive research by Underberg, local historians, and community members into an explorable virtual map of East Mims filled with digital stories and multimedia exhibits. The Folkvine project, an interdisciplinary effort across several departments at UCF, presented Central Florida folk artists and their art through the Internet.

Integration was used to accomplish the ethnographic storytelling aim of drawing readers into the stories of both sites. For example, in the East Mims project, Underberg wanted to re-create the experience of "firing the grove," which citrus workers engaged in when a freeze was coming. To bring this experience to life, two UCF undergraduate digital media students created an animated piece that illustrated the process, which was narrated by an informant in one of the oral histories.

In the same project, the ability of new media to create explorable environments provided the rationale for the design of the section on the historic Clifton Colored School. Interactivity and nonlinear narrativity enable this aspect of the community's story to be told. The visitor can enter a virtual re-creation of the historic school—built by early African American residents—and navigate through the desks inside to discover aspects of this important landmark (Underberg 2006a, 2006b).

The potential of new media to bring audiences inside cultural experiences and stories provides anthropologists—as it has others—with a powerful incentive to consider not only the possibilities offered by but also the potential costs of engaging in such work. Since the very beginning of the field, digital humanities scholars have focused their attention on the potential risks as well as benefits of using digital technology as a means for expressing human creativity. Murray (1997), for example, frames the debate in terms of the so-called utopic versus dystopic paradigms:

> The holonovel [a form of virtual reality fiction] offers a model of an art form that is based on the most powerful technology of sensory illusion imaginable but is nevertheless continuous with the larger human tradition of storytelling, stretching from the heroic bards through the nineteenth-century novelists. The feely [an interactive movie with sensations and smells] . . . offers an opposing image of a sensation-based storytelling medium that is intrinsically degrading, fragmenting, and destructive of meaning, a medium whose success implies the death of the great traditions of humanism, or even a fundamental shift in human nature itself. (Murray 1997:26)

Ethnographers, of course, are particularly sensitive to the potential and risks of new technology, and have developed insights and methodologies related to new media design and practice.

Collaborative New Media Design

As an emerging area of what Silver (2000) refers to as critical cyberculture studies, digital design studies technological decision and design processes that create the interface between network and users. In the past, the kinds of communities and identities found on the Internet were studied but less so the equally important ways in which the digital design of networked spaces creates—and restricts—particular forms of interaction. In general, digital design includes (1) hypertext studies, or how hypertext reconfigures text, writer, and reader (discussed earlier); (2) human-computer interaction (HCI), which studies interface design and its effects; and (3) participatory design (PD), in which people destined to use the system play a critical role in designing it (see, for example, Wynn 1991).

Forte (2004) locates the process of working with informants to create websites about their culture as a variant of action research—online action research. Focusing on efforts to conduct both real-world and virtual research (such as website creation) with the Santa Rosa Carib Community of Arima, Trinidad, Forte discusses how website development was used as part of a program of collaborative research. Forte argues for the use of website development as a component of collaborative research itself. Such work creates partnerships between ethnographer and research collaborators, which in turn transforms the research process (Forte 2004). Forte notes that Hine (2000) and Paccagnella (1997) are concerned with the research ethics questions raised by so-called virtual ethnography. Hine (2000) concludes that researchers need to reconceptualize research ethics as a collaborative effort between researchers and research collaborators, rather than a simple procedure in which researchers "take" and participants "give" (Hine 2000).

Such work may involve considerations of indigenous rights in relation to the use of digital technologies to represent indigenous culture, which was the subject of a 2001 report, "Indigenous Identities: Oral, Written Expressions and New Technologies" (UNESCO 2001). This report contained a section entitled "New Technology, Anthropology, Museology and Indigenous Knowledge," which included protocols for collaboration, use of multimedia for teaching and research, and the relation between transmission of traditional knowledge and ethical issues. The report outlines the mandate to provide developing countries with the information technology they need to participate actively. The report advocates the position that emerging media should help establish closer collaborations, rather than further dividing them, and that results of research should be made readily available. Among the findings of the report was the admonition to develop computer programs and databases in a language (technical and cultural) relevant to the indigenous people themselves (UNESCO 2001).

Moore and Hennessey's (2006) work with the Tagish First-Voices Project provides a useful contemporary example of how new media work with native communities can be formulated. The project is an examination of the ways indigenous communities use digital technologies for self-representation. Moore and Hennessey analyze the development of an indigenous language ideology by the website team. They argue that new media has enabled community management of the project in a way that allows for community control over self-representation. The language ideology they developed is based on an ethic of local control over language resource development. Specifically, they pursue this goal through acknowledging the authority of elders in matters of language and culture, teaching youth to become language documenters, integrating cultural traditions like the potlatch into language use and cultural representations, and making project resources free and readily available to the community (Moore and Hennessey 2006). The ready availability of digital technology facilitates the production of these community-based projects because of the increasing user friendliness of computer software and the facilitation of the interactions between community members and technical specialists.

Moore and Hennessey identify three themes at the heart of the Tagish FirstVoices language ideology, including a belief in the holistic nature of language and culture, a preference for traditional interaction styles, and the importance of acknowledging the wisdom of elders. The holistic nature of nature and culture is reflected in their project in a number of ways, including strategies of website design. The splash page shows an image of the largest Tagish-Tlingit community and features an introduction by a native Tagish speaker who refers to her lineage (Moore and Hennessey 2006).

In addition, the Tagish FirstVoices team has made an attempt to carry out their website project in a way that is consistent with traditional forms of social interaction. For example, the Tag-

ish team emphasized consensus building and continuous dialogue, which are practices in keeping with cultural ideals em-
phasizing the importance of cooperation. In addition, project
team members were integrated into the digital project in a
way consistent with "offline" forms of social interaction. They
note, for instance, that the way young people participate in the
project represents a return to their traditional role as messen-
gers to neighboring areas—with the difference that their mes-
sage relay is now lightning-quick due to the Internet (Moore and
Hennessey 2006). The third principle, the centrality of elders'
knowledge, is integrated into the project through returning control over Tagish-Tlingit cultural representation to community
elders, thus reaffirming their social worth (Moore and Hennessey 2006).

As we note in the introduction to this book, the ubiquity
and relative ease of use of computer technology has enabled
new levels of empowerment for communities in managing their
own self-representations. The ethic of "reciprocal technology"
(Underberg 2006b) strives to enable communities to have an
equal say in how their culture is portrayed by bringing them into
discussion and negotiation regarding new media representation.

In our experience, the identification of key cultural ideas that
can be used to structure new media design and interaction experiences emerges out of a process of research, listening, and
dialogue. For example, in working with Puerto Rican artist Lilly
Carrasquillo, an Orlando, Florida, folk artist, the Folkvine team
portrayed her as a member of what sociologist Jorge Duany
(1996, 2000) calls "the nation on the move" ("*la nación en vaivén*")
through acknowledgment, rather than denial, of the hybrid and
nonterritorial notions of identity that folk artists who create art
in a multicultural and transnational context may have. In other
words, rather than trying to make her story fit into established
notions of "authentic" folklore, in which a folk artist only makes
authentic traditional art when he or she learns it from another
via informal face-to-face interaction and passes it on to other
folk group members in an unbroken chain, the team worked with
the artist to conceive of an exploratory and experiential way to

present the key cultural ideas of border crossing and memory landscapes.

The integration of this key cultural idea can be seen, for example, in the design of the website's splash page. The splash page features a Mexican-style sun mask merged with mosaic tiles based on Puerto Rican Taíno Indian petroglyphs. When the user mouses over the sides of the mask, more Taíno imagery appears, providing links to the rest of the website. In this way, ancient and modern Puerto Rican and Mexican culture and artistic influences are digitally merged in a way that imitates Carrasquillo's work (Underberg 2010).

With this brief background in mind, we turn to two case studies that combine new media with anthropological interpretation. In the next chapter we present two recent projects, Folkvine.org and PeruDigital, in order to open up the interpretive process and production experience.

CHAPTER 2

Florida and Peru: Experiments in Ethnographic Representation

In recent years, scholars have increasingly turned their attention to the ways in which digital culture enables communities to express their identities. Scholars such as Moore and Hennessey (2006) and Christensen (2003) have studied the use of new technology to reassert "offline" cultural identity. Christensen's work, for example, investigates the expression of Inuit social identity online, arguing that the design of Inuit web pages reflects a self-image of peripherality, seen through, for example, the inclusion of references to physical space and boundaries such as images of Inuit in the Arctic environment and physical maps of land claim areas. Their self-representation on the Internet is characterized by the specific, local, and embodied.

As Moore and Hennessey (2006) point out, the contemporary ubiquity of digital technology enables closer interactions between technical experts and community members. If real-world cultures continue to be significant in the digital world, then, and communities can embed their culture online, the opportunity exists to use the computer medium to share cultural stories using embodied perspective and spatial navigation. This idea is in keeping with Marion and Offen's (2009) characterization of multisensory ethnography as a field engaged with feelings and the senses. It is to recent experiments in digital ethnographic representation on the Internet that we now turn (this chapter, in part, draws on ideas to be published in a forthcoming issue of *Visual Anthropology*).

Nicario Jiménez's Folkvine.org Website

Nicario Jiménez's Folkvine.org website (Folkvine.org was an interdisciplinary effort at UCF funded by the Florida Humanities Council) was Underberg and Zorn's first collaboration on integrating aspects of Andean culture into website design. Underberg and Zorn's approach resonates with Forte's (2004) call to transform the research process through collaborative partnerships between ethnographers and research collaborators.

Jiménez is an award-winning Peruvian *retablo* (portable altar) artist with whom Underberg and Zorn closely collaborated in the conceptualization and design of his website. Jiménez himself is a native of the Peruvian highland region of Ayacucho, and a native speaker of Quechua. His work incorporates both traditional Andean thought and reflections on contemporary social issues like immigration and interethnic relations, both in Peru and the United States. We sought to convey aspects of living in and being a member of Andean culture to an audience through digital ethnographic storytelling techniques (Mitchell and Charmaz 1998; Underberg 2006b).

As Underberg has argued elsewhere (2010), a collaborative research methodology allows for the identification of key cultural ideas to form the foundation for digital media design and production. In attempting to embed Andean ways of seeing and thinking into the website, we agreed to focus on two key cultural concepts: complementary duality and the tripartite division of time and space. The Andean idea of complementary duality involves a paired relationship of opposites that stand in a hierarchical relationship to each other. This complementary duality is expressed in multiple ways, such as in the idea of the idealized unity of the married pair (*chachawarmi* in Quechua). The concept of duality in general pervades Andean culture—the upper and lower, dark and light, and so forth.

The tripartite division of time and space is another key cultural idea. In Andean thought, the universe is divided into an upper world (top, or *Janaq Pacha* in Quechua), a "this" world (middle, or *Kay Pacha*), and an underworld (bottom, or *Ukhu Pacha*). The Quechua word *Pacha* is used to express both space and time, and the spatial division into three worlds relates to a time-based division in which the top is the past (*Ñawpa Pacha*, or previous), the middle is the present (*Kay Pacha*, or middle), and the bottom is the future (*Qepa Pacha*, or future).

The Andean concepts of duality and time-space relations are reflected in the folk art *retablo* form. According to Ulfe (2004), early *retablos* (referred to as the *cajón san marcos*) were divided into two sections, but more recently some artists, like Jiménez, have made them of three levels.

Including elements of the Andean worldview begins at the site's splash page, a virtual *retablo* design that contains within it and reveals three levels that correspond to Andean cosmology: the top represents the "past" (history) of *retablos*, the middle represents the "present" (artist's biography and a presentation of his *retablos*), and the bottom represents the "future" (the artist at work on his future *retablos*). Throughout the site, multimedia integration (see Packer and Jordan 2002) is used to pull the website visitor into the unfolding experience of navigating Jiménez's digital ethnographic story.

In the section devoted to the past, the user can navigate hot-linked examples of the *cajón san marcos* and the later *retablo aya-cuchano*, made by Jiménez's grandfather and father, respectively. This section of the website was created from a fieldwork photo of a shelf in Jiménez's home in Naples, Florida, on which these pieces were displayed. The website explication of the meaning of these pieces simulates the fieldwork experience of listening to Jiménez's explanation of the meaning and function of these pieces in his own family and in Andean culture more generally.

By clicking on these examples, the user is taken to a separate page that explains, in text, photo, and video explanation by Jiménez himself, the form's function and meaning. Visitors learn, for example, that the *cajón san marcos* had primarily a religious or ritual function, and can hear Jiménez talking about his father making a *cajón san marcos*. Because this form of *retablo* typically had two levels, with the top level representing the upper world of Catholic saints and the animals over which they served as patrons, and the bottom level representing the Earth and the actions of people primarily engaged in celebratory rituals, this section also introduces visitors to the Andean concept of duality. Included is information on what saints represent the patrons of which animals, and how the *cajón san marcos* was used in religious ceremonies such as the *herranza*, or ritual marking of cattle (Ulfe 2005; see also Arguedas 1958). For example, the visitor hears Jiménez explain: "They were little boxes, three-dimensional, many figures, in which scenes appear, divided into two because of the Quechua concept of duality: *hanaq pacha* (upper world) and *kay pacha* (this world-earth). This shows the presence of the two religions — Catholic and Andean."

To reinforce the visitor's awareness of the pervasiveness of this theme and the importance of complementary duality in Andean cultural thought, pictures of textiles made by Jiménez's wife are included along with a brief explanation of how women making textiles represents a complementary duality with *retablistas* who are primarily men.

As the user scrolls along the interactive bookshelf, he or she can roll over the later *retablo ayacuchano* form created by Jiménez's father. This includes learning about how the primary function of the form changed from a religious or ritual one to an artistic one, partly because of the influence of art collector Alicia Bustamante in the 1940s; Bustamante worked with artist Joaquín López Antay to expand the themes in his work to address scenes from daily life (Arguedas 1958; Ulfe 2004, 2005, 2009). In this section the visitor can learn about the *retablo ayacuchano* and see representative examples made by Jiménez's father.

Presentation of the *retablo ayacuchano* in the "Past" section of the website also serves to establish the context for understanding the work of Jiménez in the "Present" section. In the "Present" section the visitor is introduced to Jiménez's biography and interpretation of the thematic content of his work. Though focused on six of the artist's contemporary *retablos*, the "Present" section allows visitors to understand the further evolution and elaboration of the *retablo* form, which focuses on sociopolitical themes as well as elements of traditional Andean culture.

Focus on these *retablos*, including such complex works as

Migration, *Pishtaku*, *Daily Work*, and *Chicago*, permits the visitor to understand the role of border crossing and travel in his work—both in Peru and in the United States (Damian, Stein, and Jiménez Quispe 2004; Ulfe 2004). It also permits the visitor to explore ties to aspects of the Andean worldview, which are reinforced in the overall design of the website. For example, the presentation of *Migration* is couched in terms of the role of immigration, ethnic identity, and struggle, topics that resonate with other works by the artist.

The *retablo Daily Work* represents a movement forward through time as a movement from top to bottom while simultaneously addressing themes of immigration and ethnic struggle. Specifically, the *retablo* includes a portrait of three levels of work that immigrants may find upon crossing the border into the United States: agricultural (top), day labor (middle), and construction (bottom), which to Jiménez represent a movement from the most marginal type of work (e.g., picking produce) to the least marginal (construction work might last longer and pay slightly more).

The *retablo* titled *Pishtaku* is also presented in terms of how it illustrates the distinctive relation of time and space in Andean thought. The *Pishtaku* is an Andean belief character who is said to kill humans for their fat, which is used to make and power objects such as church bells and machinery, depending on the time period to which the legend corresponds. The identity of the *Pishtaku* represents forces of oppression throughout history—from the Franciscan friars represented at the top, to the twentieth-century priests making machinery in the middle, to the 1980s soldiers during the Shining Path period at the bottom; thus "reading" the *retablo* from top to bottom represents a movement forward in time, which in turn resonates with Andean cosmological thought (Canessa 2000; Ulfe 2004).

The "Future" section includes a virtual glimpse into Jiménez's workshop, where the visitor can learn more about Jiménez at work, as well as information about the materials and colors he uses. The visitor sees a video of Jiménez in his workshop, as well as photos of his workshop accompanied by textual commentary related to the materials used (including how his father developed a special slow-drying paste that allowed for more precise modeling of the figures), how Jiménez adapts his materials to the environment (moving from Lima, Peru, to Naples, Florida), and how he sees art world definitions of art and craft in relation to his own evolving work as an artist. This section also includes information about future plans for more *retablos*, such as one about the environment, thus giving the user a glimpse into the future of the form and how the themes are continually expanding and changing. Overall, the materials and their manner of presentation in this section of the website are designed to convey the process of making this form of folk art, and thus communicate how folklore is always adapting and evolving to new times, places, and the needs and desires of the individual artist.

PeruDigital

The PeruDigital project (**B**) grew out of Underberg and Zorn's collaboration on Jiménez's website and incorporates lessons Underberg learned from the production of a heritage-based computer game that will be discussed in more detail in later chapters (Underberg 2008). Now in its second phase of development (**C**), the PeruDigital project aims to present and interpret Peruvian festivals and folklore through the medium of the Internet, using archive data from the world-renowned Institute of Ethnomusicology (IDE) at the Pontifical Catholic University of Peru–Lima (PUCP), as well as materials collected by members of the UCF PeruDigital team in Florida and Peru. The project is a partnership between faculty and students at the PUCP and the UCF Digital Ethnography Lab.

The design and production of this project are made possible by a process of prototyping and evaluating the use of new media to represent Peruvian festivals through an interactive and immersive website in three languages. This involves an iterative process of design, production, and evaluation (Watkins 2007) influenced by reflexive and collaborative developments in anthropology and

Peruvian Lord of Miracles procession in Kissimmee, Florida, 2009. Courtesy: Natalie M. Underberg.

heritage studies (Giaccardi and Palen 2008; Pack 2006; Peers and Brown 2003; Pink 2001; Ruby 1980; Varese 2006) to represent cultures using technology in a collaborative manner (Underberg 2006b). Like other scholars interested in critical cyberculture studies (see Silver 2000), we focus on the potential—positive and negative—of digital media to impact human expression (see Murray 1997).

Participatory design (PD), which involves collaboration among potential users as well as among multidisciplinary scholars, is an iterative process that moves from due diligence (organizational observation, domain review, and initial project strategy) to design cycles that repeat until the system or artifact reaches its desired performance (Watkins 2007). This period of "due diligence," which allowed us to establish the foundation for the project, began in 2007–2008, with partnership-building trips by Zorn and Underberg to the PUCP to discuss ideas for collaboration, followed by selection, duplication, annotation, and interpretation of Institute of Ethnomusicology data to be used as the basis for the pilot project. Ongoing throughout the project has been the building and maintenance of an international, inter-disciplinary advisory board including cultural consultants. This resonates with Giaccardi and Palen's (2008) admonition to attend to the social and technical infrastructure of such digital cultural heritage projects; this includes establishing partnerships with "stakeholders" and obtaining and managing data assets.

The next step, the prototyping stage, involved design of the website (both visually and interactively). The PD team had two groups: digital ethnographers with cultural consultants (faculty and community members) and a technical and research production team (mainly students). The research and technical production team involved approximately fifteen students divided into discrete role-based groups: digital media production (graphic design, interactive development, video editing and production, and content asset management), ethnographic research, and translation. The PeruDigital team met monthly, with weekly subgroup meetings (production team, research team, etc.), and communicated through a project wiki. Completing this step allowed us to present a pilot to our advisory board and garner feedback to be incorporated in the design loop (**D**).

Animation professor Jo Anne Adams later joined the team as art director, and human-computer interaction (HCI) specialist Si-Jung "Jun" Kim added his expertise in formalizing the HCI research design. To help evaluate the website pilot project, a team of UCF digital media students critiqued and offered redesign ideas. Their critiques and design suggestions were included with those of the advisory board and cultural consultants in deciding on redesign priorities for the second phase of project development. The most frequently cited critique by both the advisory board and the students concerned the apparent mismatch between visual and textual style and the need to clarify the project's audience. These critiques formed the basis of the project redesign, by lead web designer and graduate student Beth Hallman, which transformed the previous vector graphics style (read as "cartoonish" and aimed only at children) into a more realistic, photographic style (**E**).

In addition to adhering to collaborative design principles and

Zorn and Underberg in Lima, Peru, on the first partnership-building trip for the PeruDigital project, 2007. Courtesy: Natalie M. Underberg.

methodology from PD and heritage studies, PeruDigital seeks to integrate anthropological and related scholarship on Peruvian culture and reflexive methodology with insights from digital media studies, including hypertext theory, transmedia story creation, and game design.

Anthropological themes such as the importance of ethnic identity, the social functions of the festival, and the historical legacies revealed in expressive culture form the foundation of the interpretive approach used in PeruDigital. Research on Peruvian festivals, popular culture, and related expressive art forms in other cultural contexts provided insights into the topics and themes, which can be explored in an immersive and interactive digital environment (Allen 2002; Arguedas 2002; Babb 1998; Bakhtin 1968; Bigenho 2002; Cánepa 2001; De La Cadena 2000; Femenías 2005, La Rosa and Mejía 2006; Mendoza 2000; Romero 1993, 2001; Turino 1993; Ulfe 2004; Underberg 2001).

In addition to anthropological themes related to Peruvian expressive culture, anthropological scholarship reflecting the increasing narrative, reflexive, and collaborative trend in folklore and anthropology is integral to the website design (Clifford and Marcus 1986; Pink 2001; Ruby 1980). The narrative approach attempts to give the overall sense of the experience, reenacting elements of the ethnographic process. Paying attention to the contemporary anthropological concern with reflexivity, as well as the role of subjectivity in understanding social experiences, we sought to find ways to embed the three perspectives of festival sponsor, performer, and ethnographer within the website interface.

Digital anthropology projects frequently consist of digitized ethnographic data and the application of markup languages. Examples include the Digital Ethnography Project (www.csus.edu /anth/researchDigitalEthnographyProject.html), which involves digitization of ethnographic and scholarly materials, but largely without the immersive and interactive interface that provides users a guided tour through those materials using anthropological interpretation. Such projects, however, are more focused on formal elements rather than on conveying information on cultural context for a general public. The objective of PeruDigital is to embed digitized content that can be explored through interaction.

This style of website design, which uses narrative and world-building techniques, is intended to augment the potential for understanding of and immersion into culture by exploiting the expressive features of new media. The project aims to use narrative techniques to adapt primary ethnographic materials into an interactive medium (Pink 2001; Titon 1995). Through nonlinear narrativity and interactivity, explorable environments have been built that aim to create point of view and a feeling of immersion (Packer and Jordan 2002).

In addition, integrating game design principles into the website allows us to experiment with combining anthropological attention to the way that subjectivity and social roles affect social experience with the expressive potential of new media to simulate cultural experience. Champion (2002) has advocated using

Screenshot of PeruDigital splash page. Courtesy: Natalie M. Underberg.

game design principles in the design and evaluation of virtual heritage projects, including role-playing, interaction with objects, and avatars. These ideas influenced the development of PeruDigital, encouraging us to develop characters, objects, and places that would allow the user to virtually experience aspects of Peruvian culture and thus engage in what Champion refers to as "cultural learning."

In the remainder of this chapter we will provide a brief walk-through of the website to illustrate how these ideas from diverse disciplines were put into practice in the design of PeruDigital. Visitors to the website are first invited to choose English, Spanish, or Quechua. They then visit a busy plaza in Lima, Peru. The Lima environment (**F**) is intended to provide introductory information about Peru, including its regions, religion, and folklore. Through interaction with objects and avatars, visitors are exposed to people, objects, and ideas that relate to specific festival environments. Here the user is introduced to the ethnomusicology student avatar, who will appear throughout the site to offer commentary on Peruvian culture; to a musician from Piura, who invites the visitor to learn more about her region by exploring the virtual ethnographer's office; and to a local vendor from the highland community of Puno, who introduces the visitor to the famous Virgin of Candelaria festival in his region.

Perusing the virtual ethnographer's office enables the user to, for example, consult ethnographic fieldwork notes on the history and meanings of the *sarahuas*, a dance/drama performed in the North Coast region of Piura, to peruse a book about the Piura region, or to view a slideshow on the desktop computer about Peruvian folklore and religion.

We have also finished a pilot of the first festival environment—the Piura, Peru, setting of the Lord of Agony festival (**G**), where visitors can learn about the festival, interact with several avatars and key objects, and learn about the performance and preparation for the festival. Interacting with the festival space exposes the visitor to issues such as ethnic and gender identity, history, and religion as they relate to the Lord of Agony festival in Afro-Peruvian North Coast Peru.

As visitors explore the Piura interactive environment, they encounter the space where the Lord of Agony statue has been richly adorned in preparation for the festival. Here the user learns about the story behind the Lord of Agony and the work of planning the

Screenshot of *serrano* (highlander) festival character in the PeruDigital interactive environment. Courtesy: Natalie M. Underberg.

festival via a notebook and dialogue from the ethnomusicology student who represents the ethnographic perspective.

In this same environment users can also explore a street scene along which the procession moves, including festival performers such as the *tamalera* (tamale seller) and a *serrano* (person from the highlands). These digital characters were based on fieldwork photographs and videos from the Institute of Ethnomusicology. For example, based on images of a figure known as the *serrano*—the person from the highlands who figures in the North Coast Lord of Agony festival—a digital character was created who in the interactive environment speaks via a dialogue box. His character wears a mask with a hat and asks repeatedly about the location of his kin ("Where is my ritual cofather?"). The visitor can view video clips of the *serrano* in character and "talk" with him and the other avatars. Helping to contextualize this stereotypical figure is another avatar or digital character who is a student at the PUCP studying ethnomusicology. He provides helpful commentary, explaining the history behind and functions of the *serrano* and other festival figures. As anthropologists and folklorists know, stereotypical figures recur in festivals worldwide, and this knowledge about how in-group identity is often formed through contrast with another group can be conveyed to the visitor.

Finally, the current Piura interactive environment contains a representation of a little girl's bedroom, a space in which videos, photos, and text are integrated into a navigable space dedicated to the performance of the *sarahuas*, a Spanish-derived dance/drama that relates to the historical conflict between the Moors and Christians in Reconquest-era Spain. This serves as a rehearsal space for the little girl who performs for the ethnographer during the festival. Within this interactive environment, for example, the visitor is able to read diary entries expressing the girl's nervous excitement about performing in the drama, watch as she "remembers" (via embedded video clips) past performances, and see her don her costume.

Finally, we have completed a curriculum for the site that enables students to adopt each of three perspectives on the festival—sponsor, performer, and ethnographer (**H**)—in order to

Screenshot of ethnomusicology student character in the PeruDigital interactive environment. Courtesy: Natalie M. Underberg.

engage in cultural learning as they explore the website. Each perspective is introduced by a brief storyline and introduction to the main character to orient the student to the primary objectives and concerns of these social roles within Peruvian culture. By seeking the answers to questions related to each of the social roles (sponsor, performer, and ethnographer), students will traverse the website in different ways, looking for different information, and will be challenged to make connections to their own lives in imitation of the social and cultural work of the people who plan, perform, and study culture.

In this chapter we have focused primarily on the ability of new media to tell a story and how collaborative methodologies can be integrated into new media project design. Next we will focus on how these same features of the digital medium can be employed to allow anthropologists to present and analyze cultural heritage materials in a way that incorporates the participatory culture of the twenty-first century.

CHAPTER 3

Digital Tools for Anthropological Analysis

Analyzing, Presenting, and Contextualizing Culture

As indicated in the introduction, the historical disconnect between anthropologists and computer technology is well known (Porter 2004). White and Truex (1998), for example, note that anthropology as a discipline has been slow to develop new software, and that it is more often than not scholars and professionals from outside the field that have encouraged computer-related developments within it.

Schwimmer (1996), similarly, expressed doubt that anthropologists would heed the call to become more involved with computer technology, noting that only a handful of anthropology departments had even established significant web presence. Zeitlyn and Houtman (1996) argue that cyberculture studies generally has been regarded by anthropologists as a discrete subdiscipline and that anthropologists have not paid sufficient attention to the effects of computer technology on the field. They draw a parallel between this and the way that visual anthropology was regarded as a separate subfield to the relative exclusion of attention to the way film and photography impacted anthropology as a whole.

The degree to which anthropologists and other social scientists need to know about computer technology and work with computer specialists (who tend to understand as much about anthropologists as many anthropologists understand about computer science) is a recurring question in several works from the 1980s and 1990s, such as Brent and Anderson's *Computer Applications in the Social Sciences* (1990), which raises the question. This work contains sections on both communicating with computer scientists and maintaining awareness of the social consequences of the computer. The book addresses both sides of the discourse on computer technology and anthropology; namely, that anthropologists need to become more versed in and comfortable with computers and, at the same time, that "social science researchers are among those who are best trained to investigate the social effects of computers" (Brent and Anderson 1990:8).

Despite this disconnect between anthropologists and computer scientists, some anthropologists and other social scientists have been developing computer tools for data analysis since the early 1980s. Sproull and Sproull (1982), for example, addressed strategies for coding interview and observational data (see also Agar 1983; Bernard and Evans 1983; Podolevsky and McCarthy 1983; Podolevsky 1987). Later computer programs such as HyperResearch were developed and adopted by ethnographers to enable multimedia analysis—especially useful for visual anthropology and related fields (Hesse-Biber, DuPuis, and Kinder 1997).

Zeitlyn and Houtman (1996) argue that computers not only radically change how ethnographers can collect and manipulate data, but also potentially enable new forms of analysis that would not be possible otherwise. Barkin and Stone (2004), for example, advocate using a "website model" of anthropological record keeping. This involves arranging data in website form, although a private and not publicly accessible one—something like a password-protected wiki. They write that anthropologists are increasingly using web page editors to organize fieldwork data such as photo, sound, and other files into one place that can then be reviewed as a single, unified text rather than remaining separated by medium. Barkin and Stone also view the integration of text and multimedia as a way to better enable the "intuitive relationships between image, sound, and word" that traditional methods of dealing with data may miss (205).

The computer's ability to store, search, retrieve, and distribute vast amounts of information, then, allows for new ways to document and link information. What such an approach enables, ultimately, is the contextualization of data in new ways. As Barkin and Stone (2004) explain, their "website model" allows the contextualization of video, images, and audio into written descriptions and interpretations. They argue that this approach enables the production of a richer ethnographic document that can be drawn on later in the interpretive process by allowing simultaneous review of descriptions and interpretation alongside multimedia ethnographic documentation. They note that this approach is quite different from that offered by most qualitative analysis software, which instead sorts out and takes out of context data elements to allow researchers to search for data elements with similar codes or topics. Instead of classifying or cross-labeling pieces of fieldwork data, this approach attempts to integrate them in a holistic manner. This strategy, they assert, enables a different sort of analysis, one that preserves the context and allows for a review of entire events in as detailed and broadly inclusive form as possible.

Beyond harnessing the encyclopedic power of the computer (Murray 1997) for ethnographic data analysis, presentation of anthropological information, and maintenance of contextual information (Molicnik 1999; Redding 1999; Schwimmer 1996), anthropologists have also used the computer to develop new ways to present anthropological scholarship itself (Stone 1998). Zeitlyn (1998), for example, notes that hypertext can make the process of arriving at conclusions more explicit. He focuses on projects at the Centre for Social Anthropology and Computing that integrate hypertext into anthropological scholarship, including the Virtual Institute of Mambila Studies and the Experience Rich Anthropology project (lucy/ukc.ac.uk/HEFCE/). Schwimmer (1997), meanwhile, argues that the computer medium allows for new forms of nonlinear computer-based ethnographic writing that can ameliorate challenges to the ethnographic representation characteristic of traditional print forms.

Surveying web-based scholarship in anthropology and anthropology projects online, Barkin and Stone (2000) indicate that few such projects at the time of their study were taking advantage of hypermedia. They note that online anthropological scholarship was typically in the form of PDFs of published articles. They also discuss how nonrefereed scholarship is "blurring the boundaries" in pedagogy. For example, graduate student research is used for teaching and research tools, such as Richard Wilk's Theory in Anthropology site. Book authors use websites to post data and illustrations; websites may even serve as a stand-alone resource. John Kanter's Sipapu website includes such materials as 3-D architectural reconstructions of Anasazi dwellings and a scholarly database of archaeological sites. Barkin and Stone single out *Current Anthropology* as an example of peer-reviewed anthropological scholarship that offers significant content online that does not appear in print. *Current Anthropology*, they argue, illustrates the four potential innovations in web-based scholarship: media enhancements such as improved imagery, structural linkage including using hyperlinks to references, ancillary materials such as inclusion of sound files, and the incorporation of subsequent scholarship through ongoing updating of the list of articles published after the original article's publication date (see also Brown 2003 for a discussion of creating a website companion to an anthropological book).

Related to innovations in presenting anthropological scholarship, recent work in digital cultural heritage encourages ethnographers to take seriously the computer medium's potential for multivocality in decentering the knowledge and authority of the scholar. The goal for the digital cultural heritage expert, then, is to construct rich knowledge environments that include space for a plurality of meanings. This requires going beyond selecting relevant items for a web-based exhibition to exploit the technical capacity of the computer to enable new search, visualization, and navigation models. Cameron and Robinson (2007) note the potential for developing innovative interpretations of museum collections by digitally incorporating multiple media, including three-dimensional visualizations, thus removing documentation from the "straightjacket" of linear narrative description. They call for archivists and curators to consider the potential for theoretical concepts like polysemic interpretive models to change the way they document and present collections.

Cameron and Robinson (2007) also advocate adopting an "epistemic relativist" paradigm in which empirical collection records are validated but augmented with alternative forms of documentation, analysis, and interpretation. For example, 3-D imaging and oral testimonies would be included in this model as an integral part of the collection, and nonspecialist would be juxtaposed with specialist interpretation. Contextualizing cultural heritage materials can be facilitated through automation systems that link objects to relevant people, places, multimedia, and so on (Cameron and Robinson 2007).

Cultural heritage experts working in museums are now seeking new ways for scholarly information to coexist with other interpretations. Museum administrators are working to create a more dynamic form of intellectualism that includes space for communication and negotiation between scholars, practitioners, educators, and source communities. This trend toward democratization may effectively reframe processes of collections development and access. Newly emerging museum practice advocates a constructivist paradigm in which learners internally construct knowledge, and learning itself refers to the individual construction of meaning.

Accompanying this constructivist paradigm is an appreciation for what digital cultural heritage theorists call "a polysemic knowledge model." Polysemic knowledge models place objects within richly constructed contexts, including source materials, websites, and exhibitions, as well as enabling user-generated interpretations. Such an approach expands and extends objects' possible meanings, and enables new methods of retrieval—which in turn necessitates new methods for dealing with and standardizing this metadata.

These constructivist and polysemic paradigms, of course, emerge more generally from the ubiquity of participatory culture today. Social networking software—think of wikis, blogs, and so on—allows for greater user participation as well as the establishment and maintenance of new forms of social connection. In this participatory culture, users contribute information, opinions, and multimedia content to existing digital projects and, increasingly, their participation is constitutive of the project itself (De Lusenet 2007).

In order to construct these participatory environments for cultural heritage preservation aims, however, scholars, computer scientists, and community participants need to be able to communicate and collaborate. Crane et al. (2005) note the importance of content experts, language technology developers, and end users all working together to learn from each other in the development of digital tools for cultural heritage preservation. They focus on evaluating a number of technologies that have potential for advancing cultural heritage preservation aims, including visualizations (such as a search-result-visualization program that clusters documents into related groups using keyword analysis) and web/XML information retrieval (analyzing the pros and cons of structured markup as undertaken by projects such as the text encoding initiative [TEI]).

Cognizant of Crane et al.'s (2005) call for humanities scholars and computer scientists to work together, UCF content experts and technological specialists have been collaborating on several related projects. In the next chapter we explore three UCF projects that utilize the extensible markup language (XML) and database development to advance the aims of ethnographic data analysis and cultural heritage preservation and dissemination.

CHAPTER 4

Using the Extensible Markup Language in Cultural Analysis and Presentation

NATALIE UNDERBERG AND RUDY MCDANIEL

Insights about using the extensible markup language (XML) can be used to assist cultural heritage research in a variety of ways. In an earlier publication (McDaniel and Underberg 2007), we briefly explained the nature and potential usefulness of XML for humanities and social science research involving narrative:

> Metadata is data about data, or descriptive data that is intended to describe or represent preexisting data from another source. Such data does not need to be visible to the user; in fact, metadata is often invisible and works behind the scenes in much the same fashion as hypertext markup language, or HTML. XML is one such metadata classification system that is derived from SGML (the same parent language of HTML) . . . It is no surprise that the next generation Semantic Web is being created based on the foundational elements of XML. Using XML as a metadata system on the Internet can lead to more relevant searches and substantially improved online experiences for a user . . . Rather than simply performing a keyword search for matching keywords, a search engine would be able to perform the additional task of seeking out content based on semantic anchors. This process involves looking for examples of the usage of the words in the context in which they were originally intended. (58)

XML emerged as part of the overall development of humanities computing, concerned as it was for expanding the potential usefulness of a digital collection beyond that of the original researcher's intentions. One major project in the developing field of humanities computing has been the text encoding initiative (TEI), which began in 1987 and developed a widely used XML version of its own (Hockey 2006). XML works by embedding tags within the document that identify relevant features within that document. It is up to the designer to identify the particular features encoded and the relation between them. XML is particularly useful for humanities and cultural anthropology computing because it enables multiple forms of processing, providing a flexible way to encode aspects of textual structure. Hockey offers the TEI example of using XML to identify structural division like chapters, sections, speeches, and so forth, to enable the researcher to retrieve and analyze all speeches by Ophelia in *Hamlet*. XML is also particularly useful in the humanities because of its ability to imitate the work of humanities scholars themselves. As Hockey explains, XML has the potential to more accurately reflect what researchers desire to do. For example, many researchers may want to directly access a particular part of a document rather than having to wade through the entire piece. XML links can utilize XML-based structures embedded within the document itself to enable more precise linking (to a single chapter, for instance). These links can then be stored external to the document and provide researchers with particular paths through the document (Hockey 2006). In the digital humanities, a well-known example is the Perseus Project at Tufts.

XML is important for digital ethnography because of the nature of digital information itself. XML is flexible and able to be manipulated in multiple ways. It has grown considerably in popularity in the digital humanities particularly for those full text sources encoded according to the TEI. XML allows specific details within documents to be presented, interpreted, and manipulated, as well as making it easier to "chunk" and integrate both data and metadata—resulting in innovative publication forms that make use of the distinctive features of the medium, such as its capacity to enable multiple paths through information and its ability to provide more robust context for that information (Cameron and Robinson 2007; Hockey 2006). The key is to take advantage of the potential afforded by the digital medium to enact cultural analysis, much like hypertext ethnography (discussed earlier), which exploits the features of digital environments to tell a story.

In the 1990s archives and libraries became interested in the delivery of digital resources rather than simply creating catalogs or finding aids for those resources. Publishers had also begun making journals available digitally, but with an eye more toward delivery rather than manipulation or analysis. Digital media was conceived of more as a communication than a computational medium (Hockey 2006). The use of XML in digital ethnography today allows us to go beyond delivery of resources to enable analysis and manipulation.

In addition, the strong emphasis on linking and connections in the humanities, which is facilitated by the use of XML, also enhances digital ethnography. Sharing these links—the vision of founders of the digital field like Vannevar Bush—enables ethnographic resources to be reusable and allows future potential users to access the thought processes that went into organizing and curating the collection in the first place.

This chapter examines how XML is being used in three such projects at UCF that represent collaborations between computer science and ethnographic experts: an analysis of personal narratives of Catholic nuns; the creation of an online portal to share resources and facilitate dialogue between digital humanities scholars and educational game makers and users; and the creation of an online portal to share the digitized newspaper stories from the pioneering Central Florida Hispanic newspaper *La Prensa*, along with the stories, photographs, and memories of Puerto Ricans throughout the diaspora and the interpretations of scholars and community members who are familiar with the events covered. This work follows Crane et al.'s (2005) call for increased communication and collaboration between scholars, technical experts, and community members. After briefly introducing each project, we discuss the use of XML in achieving ethnographic and cultural heritage research aims.

Introduction to the Projects

In the first collaboration, which we refer to as "exembellishment" (McDaniel and Underberg 2007), we used sample vocation narratives from Underberg's ethnographic fieldwork with southern US and Peruvian nuns to suggest an XML framework for coding and displaying narratives from a particular storytelling community in a digitized format (McDaniel and Underberg 2007). In this type of work, we advocate using the potential of XML to assign meaningful metadata (descriptive data) to narrative. We argue that by creating metatags and assigning them to narrative documents, researchers are better able to research and solicit new stories from specific storytelling communities. Using XML is particularly useful because it can allow one to pattern story scripts based on what are called "document type definitions" (DTDs).

The second project, the Digital Humanities Exchange (DHE) initiative, builds on work by ourselves and other colleagues at UCF on video games in the humanities. It is designed to share what we have learned with other educators and researchers and facilitate exchange between expert/amateur, artist/scholar, and teacher/student within the domain of games-based learning. The project, in its development phase, consists of an interactive community-driven web portal to manage digital assets that can be used in scholarly game-based learning contexts. This portal functions as a trading post where pioneering scholars can exchange ideas, assets, and knowledge of best practices for using game-based learning in the humanities. The DHE includes the Turkey Maiden Educational Computer Game, a computer game mod (a modification of an existing computer game engine) project directed by Underberg, designed to teach about Central Florida history and culture (discussed in more detail later in the book).

The third project, entitled Digital Diaspora, is intended to create an online portal to share the digitized collection of *La Prensa*, the pioneering Hispanic newspaper founded in Central Florida in 1981, and enable the creation of a public archive related to the events and topics documented in this historically significant newspaper. This project is in the initial stages of development.

Using XML to Analyze Cultural Information

In "Exembellishment: Using the eXtensible Markup Language as a Tool for Storytelling Research" (McDaniel and Underberg 2007), we point out how ideas from folkloristics can inform the development and use of this digital media tool. We suggest that the term *normalform* can be useful for digital storytelling researchers, distinguishing as it does the basic framework for a particular type of folk narrative (Georges and Jones 1995). While for many years folklorists primarily concerned themselves with traditional narratives such as the European folktale, the legend, or the myth, more recently they have turned their analytical eye toward discerning formulas and patterns in personal narratives (see Stahl 1989).

Underberg was able to identify the sociohistorical context that gave rise to the development and performance of a particular genre of personal narrative, the vocation narrative, among Benedictine nuns who entered religious life beginning in the 1980s in two historically related communities, and to identify the underlying structure of the narrative form that was common to all informants.

Very briefly, this development of a longer, more conflict-oriented vocation narrative shared by those entering religious life in these communities resulted from a vocational crisis brought on by the changes to religious life mandated in the 1960s by the

Street scene in Morropón, Peru, home of one of the communities of Benedictine sisters who shared their vocation stories with Underberg. Courtesy: Natalie M. Underberg.

Second Vatican Council. As in many such communities, nearly half of the nuns left the convent under study during the turbulent late 1960s and early 1970s, which resulted in a growing need for more people to join their order. Unlike the elder sisters in the community, who largely grew up in the vicinity of the convent and demonstrated their likely "calling" to religious life through such externally observable activities as frequent attendance at Mass and an expressed desire to be like the nuns/teachers they admired, the newer entrants to the community tend to be older, come from farther away, and to possess different background experiences from those of the existing convent members. The upshot was that, in the 1980s, an aggressive and media savvy marketing campaign was developed to secure new entrants for a community that was in danger of dying out. Thanks to the business acumen and hard work of the sisters and their advisors, the number of vocations to their community eventually grew, in part because of the ability of aspiring entrants to tell a compelling personal narrative about their call to religious life that would be recognized and legitimated as valid by the nuns of the community they wanted to join.

In our project, we used the unique seven-part structural outline of a *normalform* for telling a convincing vocation narrative as the set of metatags in XML. To put it in folkloristic—and narratological—terms, the *normalform* of the story, consisting of seven elements, provides the syntagmatic structure for these stories; the crucial part played by discernment (or determining the will of God through prayer and silence) indicates something about the paradigmatic structure of the narratives (see Lévi-Strauss 1969):

1. the receipt of a call and resistance to that call
2. surrender to the call as an account of the first successful listening to God
3. determination of the validity of the call to religious life in general
4. the narrowing of a general call to a particular subtype of religious life
5. realization of the call to the Ferdinand/Morropón Benedictines
6. the facing and overcoming of obstacles following acceptance of the call
7. the identification of the time of entrance into the order and a statement of contentment with the call

At the core of these stories is an opposition between being willing versus being unwilling to listen; the working out of this conflict serves as a gatekeeping mechanism regulating acceptance into the community (McDaniel and Underberg 2007). Identifying both levels of narrative structure—syntagmatic and paradigmatic—can be used to create meaningful XML coding, which can in turn help researchers better identify, elicit, and display these narratives and their contextual meanings.

XML can also usefully clarify ambiguity within texts. XML can thus help narrative researchers dealing with more complex narratives, enabling them to conduct more precise searches on narratives in a given database. For example, they would be able to search not only for keywords but also for specific aspects of keywords—such as with the use of an <event> tag to relate important events within a particular type of story. Such a system could help create smarter searches, in which tags are stored in grouped units accompanied by meaningful related words that provide needed contextual information (McDaniel and Underberg 2007).

We explain how this potential of XML tags for providing semantic meaning to the narrative would work in the case of the vocation narrative:

> Particular tags such as <obstacle> and <call_realization> enable researchers to compare and contrast new stories based solely on the *normalform* of preexisting vocation stories in the database. After this set of tags has been applied, it is relatively easy to create a simple Internet search engine script to parse and control search results based on keyword searches. A user can now search for very specialized information within a story collection; for example "search all vocation stories where location = X, obstacle = Y, and the call narrowing sequence contains keyword Z" would be a perfectly valid search, and would likely return quite accurate results given a large enough set of stories to search through. (McDaniel and Underberg 2007:66)

By beginning with an XML coding of a particular narrative, we hope to contribute to the creation of a narrative research system that enables improved searching and classification of this type of narrative.

Facilitating Exchange: A Database for Sharing Assets for Educational Computer Game Design

As indicated earlier, the objective of the Digital Humanities Exchange (DHE) project is to facilitate the exchange of information, materials, and assets related to educational computer game design. Although the DHE is open to non-heritage-based games, we will focus here on how the DHE can help cultural heritage experts gain and share information and materials. As mentioned earlier, one of the games included in the DHE is the Turkey Maiden Educational Computer Game mod, a game based on a Spanish folktale collected in Depression-era Ybor City, Florida, the historic "Cigar Capital of the World" and home to Spanish, Cuban, and Italian immigrant communities. Turkey Maiden is a mod of the popular role-playing game NeverWinter Nights. The DHE makes available assets from the game itself, the curriculum, and the primary historical materials used in the creation of the game, such as historical photographs and documents related to 1930s Ybor City.

Mods are the current focus of the Turkey Maiden project because they offer a way for instructors to create computer games for educational purposes without having to build a game engine from scratch (see Koster 2004 and Pearce, Witten, and Barti 2006 for a discussion of the potential of modding to allow players and nonprofessional game designers to customize the game). David Leonard (2006) notes the predominance of white player characters in commercial games and of racial and ethnic stereotypes when nonwhite player characters are included, suggesting the need for game experiences that more responsibly address issues of cultural diversity. Educational computer game mods offer educators the opportunity to construct game characters and worlds that celebrate cultural diversity in a way that is compatible with educational goals related to history and heritage. For example, Turkey Maiden incorporates Federal Writers' Project Works Progress Administration (WPA) materials (available through the University of South Florida's library), historic photographs, and newspaper stories on Ybor City into a game story that takes students on a folktale-inspired educational tour through Depression-era Ybor City.

The DHE portal is intended to enable teachers, humanities scholars (including cultural anthropologists), and others to apply the ideas of cultural learning embedded in the Turkey Maiden game into their own projects (discussed in more detail later in the book), thus using technology to enable (enact) cultural analysis. Integrating these insights into the DHE demonstrates how scholars and others can combine original source materials with the newest technologies. The project, to culminate in a "trading post" for scholars, will facilitate scholarly dialogue and share information about how educational computer games can be built—even with scarce resources. The project is intended to be a contribution to interdisciplinary information management, using the same kinds of complex visualization systems and resource management interfaces that are seen in contemporary virtual worlds.

The DHE also relates to a problem that is currently the focus of much research in the digital humanities: how to deal effectively with the proliferation of data that characterizes the digital world today. With so much information, more and more sophisticated methods for sorting through that information in meaningful ways become necessary. It is in this niche that humanities work—and the closely related field of cultural anthropology—figures. Finally, the integration of scholarly dialogue through discussion forums and mechanisms for feedback will enable creative new approaches to combining expert knowledge, scholarly skills, and project assets. Such an approach contributes to the creation of a constructivist model in which new media users are less passive consumers than consumers/producers, and tallies with De Lusenet's (2007) argument that, in today's so-called participatory culture, user contributions are fundamental to the creation of the project itself.

DHE is modeled on resources like TurboSquid (www.turbo squid.com), but geared toward a more scholarly audience. Specifically, the DHE will combine the technological capacities of a resource management system with scholarly discussion and integration of humanities-oriented primary source materials. Similar projects include Valley of the Shadows and Explore Art (Himalayan art). The portal will also use open-source technologies such as Apache and XML to design the system, so that knowledge and assets can be traded among users.

The asset management system used in the DHE will be combined with collaborative tools and threaded discussion forums. The portal itself is intended to contain digital files from games, including 3-D models and digitized source materials (such as the

Depression-era Federal Writers' Project WPA materials used in the Turkey Maiden game), that are described in terms of both scholarly contextual information and potential practical uses in the games. Scholars will code project files and assets, and then public access will be enabled; this in turn will enable additional contextual meanings to be assigned to the assets by users of the portal.

In particular, the storage and access aspect of the project is relevant to the humanities because it will enable user access to humanities assets that may be 3-D (like 3-D models) or otherwise better encountered in a 3-D environment than in a linear archive or database (such as one that only involves texts). This will in turn allow users to find out more about how issues related to culture, identity, and history can be explored within a game (e.g., enabling the player to adopt more than one avatar or digital character's perspective).

Further, a portal is being developed so that it can be searched according to narrative parameters such as the sociocultural context of the creation of the asset and the time of its creation. This unique system will allow users to search for content along content- and context-based lines, that is, according to both asset descriptions and historical or cultural significance of events related to the assets.

In practical terms, the DHE is being built using five technologies: (1) a relational database system and server-side scripting language (such as PHP); (2) technical expert-generated metadata to describe file formats and potential uses; (3) expert-generated subject matter metadata to describe the sociocultural significance of special collections; (4) social classification systems to provide user-generated tags for linking and extending archive materials (e.g., Flickr); and (5) threaded discussion boards to facilitate scholarly and producer discussions related to the contents, meanings, and uses of the database. Thus far, we have set up the high-capacity server to house the project and completed the programming and development of a prototype web-based system that is intended to serve as an initial test phase for the portal.

Digital Diaspora: *La Prensa* and the Recuperation of Collective Memory

The Digital Diaspora project is intended to leverage the community wisdom accrued through the creation of an oral history archive to augment the knowledge encapsulated in the Central Florida newspaper *La Prensa* in a way that brings together the insights and perspectives of humanities scholars with members of the public in a forum that encourages dialogue and discussion. Such an approach follows Cameron and Robinson's (2007) admonition to utilize electronic culture's ability to reframe scholarly authority with multiple meanings. Specifically, the project will involve four components: digitizing the newspapers; making them searchable according to metatags determined in consultation with humanities scholars (significant events, people, and themes); enabling the submission of stories, photos, and commentary from the public that relate to the newspaper stories and the events, people, and themes they document; and interpretations of the historical events on the part of scholars and participants.

This project builds on fieldwork among Latin Americans in Central Florida that was conducted by Underberg in 2003–2004 and in 2008–2009. In 2008–2009, Underberg and team collected more than seventy-five oral history interviews and hundreds of photographs from Puerto Ricans who had settled in Central Florida in the last fifty years. This project resulted in a 2-D (text panel) and digital story exhibit (**I**). The project also incorporates McDaniel's ideas for using XML (see, for example, McDaniel and Underberg 2007).

Digital Diaspora is important for several reasons. The Puerto Rican population in Central Florida is booming, and Puerto Ricans have played a significant part in building the Central Florida region through the establishment of institutions such as social clubs (e.g., La Asociación Borinqueña), cultural celebrations (e.g., the Puerto Rican parade), and journalism (e.g., *La Prensa*). The growth of the Puerto Rican population in Central Florida has been dramatic, increasing from approximately

100,000 in 1980 to more than 700,000 in 2007. In fact, the number of Puerto Ricans in Florida is second only to that in New York within the fifty US states, and the greatest increase in this Puerto Rican population from 1990 to 2000 occurred in Florida (an increase of 241,354). By far the main destination of Puerto Rican migrants from between 2000 and 2006 was been Orange County, Florida (nearly 35,000). These so-called Disney Ricans have made a significant impact on the social, economic, and political landscape of Central Florida (Duany 2009).

The Puerto Rican experience has been characterized by what sociologist Jorge Duany calls *la nación en vaivén*, or "the nation on the move" (Duany 1996, 2000). Duany uses this phrase to describe the fluid and hybrid identities characteristic of contemporary Puerto Ricans. He encourages scholars to consider the social rather than merely physical spaces in which Puerto Ricans live, and how they create cultural meaning in the diaspora. The project explores the possibility of the Internet to enable the creation and sharing of hybrid identities online (Christensen 2003; Underberg 2006b, 2010; see also García Canclini 1995 for an important discussion of cultural hybridity from the perspective of Latin American studies). With this project we have the opportunity to bring together official and unofficial accounts of important historical events along with the memories and experiences of people who have intersected with these events and may live in diverse communities throughout the diaspora. This project enables us to raise the question: Can the Internet become a space for reconstruction of the Puerto Rican "imaginary" (Flores 2000)?

In order to facilitate a sense of distributed community among Latin Americans residing across the fifty US states, we plan to use Web 2.0 technologies to build an interactive web portal with access to digitized documents from *La Prensa* as well as the oral histories collected from Central Florida Puerto Ricans. The digitized collection will be annotated using searchable metadata that is then further cross-referenced to oral histories collected from Puerto Ricans living in Central Florida from the 1940s to the late 1980s. For the period from 1981 to 1987, official historical records from *La Prensa* can be compared to individual oral his-

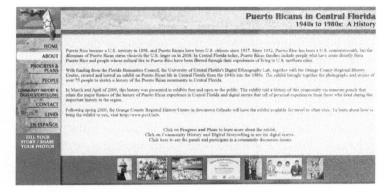

Puerto Ricans in Central Florida, 1940s–1980s: A History website homepage.
Courtesy: Natalie M. Underberg.

tories and accounts from Central Florida residents of that same period. Additional accounts from individuals who have migrated to other areas of the United States will be collected using online bulletin boards and web forms in order to provide a mechanism for bridging different diasporic communities (particularly in regions like New York, New Jersey, Orlando, and Miami).

Web 2.0 generally relies heavily on social networking and user feedback in order to build a sense of community online. Examples include Facebook, YouTube, and Twitter. In this sense, individuals not geographically co-located can still participate in an online community and participate in and contribute to an online scholarly community based on official historical documents and community stories important to Latin American heritage. Also characteristic of Web 2.0 technologies is the lack of centralized planning (of content) and the emergent and organic growth of the virtual sites based largely on community feedback and participation. In this sense, we will build the foundations of the web portal, and the source scholarly content (*La Prensa* digitized content and the transcribed oral histories and recordings) will act as catalysts for discussion and further contribution of materials from community members.

This process enables a more democratic means of engaging

with source materials and contributing to archival collections. Robert Glenn Howard refers to the category of online discourse made possible through Web 2.0 technologies as the "vernacular web." The vernacular is, by definition, different from the institutional, and serves to call upon an alternate form of authority. He writes that "the concept of a vernacular web provides the theoretical language necessary for speaking about the complex hybridity that new communication technologies make possible" (Howard 2008:192; see also Bolter 2001 and Landow 2006 for a discussion of hypertext's potentially democratizing features). In their introduction to the collection *Democracy and New Media*, editors Henry Jenkins and David Thorburn (2004) note the contrast between older "consensus" forms of media broadcasting and newer technologies for information dissemination that function "according to principles fundamentally different from those of broadcast media: access, participation, reciprocity, and many-to-many rather than one-to-many communication" (Jenkins and Thorburn 2004:2). In this new media economy, the importance of source materials is augmented by the rich contributions of community members, who annotate, extend, challenge, or otherwise shape the new content according to their own insights or perspectives. This is an important feature of social networking technologies and also a central part of Digital Diaspora; this feature seeks to adopt an "epistemic relativist" position as outlined by Cameron and Robinson (2007). This project, in addition to allowing users to comment on source materials and upload new documents for discussion, will feature a mechanism for registering accounts and searching for users based on particular demographic data. The site will also feature a privacy option for those contributors who do not wish to have their profiles accessible to general users.

From a narrative perspective, the implementation of user-generated strategies for sharing personal stories is an interesting research topic because it combines the benefits of flexible hypertext technologies with first-person perspective accounts authored by individuals with ties to historical events. The official reported versions of newspaper articles can be juxtaposed with the personal accounts of those in attendance during covered events, for example. This will be done using hyperlinks leading from the digitized source materials and custom XML tags that are associated with the personal histories collected from that time period.

Digital Diaspora is intended to draw on a rich lived experience in Florida and the diaspora, and bring together around a unique archive (*La Prensa*) humanities scholars with people who lived the experiences recorded in its pages. We believe this project provides a unique opportunity to use Web 2.0 technologies to address a humanities question of great importance to Latin American studies, specifically, the way that diasporic communities are created and maintained. This project allows us to ask: Can the Internet become a space for creating diasporic communities?

Many researchers working with historical collections recognize the ubiquity, accessibility, and pervasiveness of digital information. In several past projects, content has been organized according to a particular theme, such as the American Civil War theme used in the Valley of the Shadows hypermedia archive at the Virginia Center for Digital History at the University of Virginia, or the Rubin Museum of Art's Explore Art online art exhibit. Others continue work in more ambitious metadata classification systems for the humanities; the Perseus Project at Tufts University is one such example. In addition, we take a cue from such projects as the New York Blackouts at Brown University, which combined archive with oral history research to reconstruct the history of the New York blackouts of 1965 and 1977. Such projects (ours included) raise questions about the verifiability of oral history research when the Internet is involved, and one of the larger research questions to be addressed by our project concerns how to deal with the potential for deception by anonymous participants.

In practical terms, completing a project like this requires several steps of development and collaboration between technical and cultural experts. The first stage, as with all such projects, involves planning and research in order to identify appropriate portal technologies (such as Drupal) and metadata classification systems; then, a small portion of articles must be selected from the extensive newspaper archives (approximately fifteen) to be digitized; an equal number of oral history excerpts must be transcribed or otherwise prepared for the portal.

The next stage involves digitization and translation, which includes digitization and metadata annotation of documents. Documents will be digitized using optical character recognition (OCR) and corrected by hand. The documents will be translated into English and offered in both Spanish and English for online display. At the same time, the server will be set up with the portal software, and a prototype architecture will be tested to house the document collection.

The third stage is that of encoding, in which the digitized documents will be uploaded to the portal site and annotated using appropriate XML data. At this point corollaries will be identified between *La Prensa* articles of particular thematic interest (e.g., historical, religious, political, cultural, etc.) that may be used as catalysts for inspiring participation from different diasporic communities situated in key geographic areas. Stories added by the community will not be tagged with metadata, but will be linked to the tagged articles using appropriate linked keys in the database tables. This will allow for a realistic rollout of the portal while still connecting these stories and events to the community. This could potentially be a considerable amount of information. These user-added stories will be subsequently annotated and tagged at a later date, if time permits.

When these steps are completed, we will have a prototype launch, which will involve launching a prototype community by mailing publicity materials to press and community contacts identified through research and contacts. As part of the massive publicity campaign necessary to launch in order to develop a vibrant and active online community to create and support the project, the publicity materials will encourage participants to visit the portal and view these Central Florida historical documents as well as to upload their own personal documents and initiate online conversations and make connections in the community. After survey feedback has been gathered from initial users, the web portal will be modified as necessary before the final step: final release (and continued support).

So far in this book we have investigated new media's ability to tell a story, considered models for collaborative research, and explored the use of digital media to present, manipulate, and analyze cultural information in a way that reconfigures the relation between author and audience, expert and layperson. In the final chapters, we discuss issues surrounding and strategies for teaching about culture using insights from virtual heritage and video game studies.

CHAPTER 5

Using Features of Digital Environments to Enable Cultural Learning

Virtual Worlds and the Virtual Human

From the beginning of the study of cyberspace, anthropologists have struggled to articulate how this new world might cause us to rethink what it means to be human and to live in a culture. Escobar's classic "Welcome to Cyberia: Notes on the Anthropology of Cyberculture" (1994) called on anthropologists to concern themselves with "cultural constructions and reconstructions on which the new technologies are based and which they in turn help to shape. The point of departure of this inquiry is the belief that any technology represents a cultural invention, in the sense that it brings forth a world; it emerges out of particular cultural conditions and in turn helps to create new ones" (Escobar 1994:211).

For Escobar, anthropological inquiry would be structured around such considerations as exploring cybercultural discourses and practices; studying these discourses and practices in particular settings; understanding the background, including modern practices, that give rise to these new technologies; and interrogating the political economy of cyberculture (see also Gelleri 2001; Miller and Slater 2001).

Fischer (1999), meanwhile, argues that ethnographers needed to attend to such issues as theory, time, place, languages, and institutions in relation to cyberspace. Cyberspace ethnography, then, presents a test for a multidimensional approach that can bring into focus such diverse concerns related to, for example, cyberspace culture, information sciences, and social impact. One of Fischer's major assertions about the way in which cyberspace changes our experience as humans is that it changes our communication and perception from one based on direct experience to one primarily mediated through technology (what he calls "technological prosthesis").

More recently, Boellstorff (2008) has conducted fieldwork inside Second Life, using his avatar and working from his virtual home and office. In contrast to those who claim that online culture announces the arrival of the "posthuman," he argues that a virtual world like Second Life is profoundly human. For Boellstorff, a term like "virtually human" has two meanings: (1) our real-world lives have always been, in a sense, virtual, and (2) in virtual worlds we are nearly—but not entirely—human, meaning that our humanity is constructed via emerging possibilities for subjectivity, community, and place. He writes:

> Anthropology . . . can help reveal the layers of contingency within which the category of the virtually human, rather than exiling such contingency into a category of the posthuman and thereby retrenching the borders of the human itself . . . Ethnography has a special role to play in studying virtual worlds because it has *anticipated* them. Virtual before the Internet existed, ethnography has always produced a kind of virtual knowledge . . . Representations of persons in virtual worlds are known as "avatars"; Malinowski's injunction to "imagine yourself" in an unfamiliar place underscores how anthropology has always been about avatarizing the self, standing virtually in the shoes . . . of another culture. (Boellstorff 2008:5–6)

Digital Cultural Heritage and Spatial Engagement

The potential of cyberspace to enable virtual worlds inhabited by virtual beings has influenced developments in recent digital cultural heritage work in ways that may be of particular interest to cultural anthropologists. Some scholars have conceived of the digital cultural heritage enterprise in terms of tourism — involving exploration and mastery over spaces. Kenderdine (2007) refers to the virtual tourist as a cyber *flâneur* (Charles Baudelaire's term), a kind of wandering sampler of local life who transforms the city space through his or her imagination and perceptions. The act of navigation, then, helps to create a virtual and subjective space. Kenderdine argues that we should develop virtual heritage spaces with the potential to creatively adapt the criteria for "presence" (including "cultural presence") to incorporate elements of narrative and virtual interactions, with the goal of engendering cultural heritage appreciation and education (Kenderdine 2007).

Increasingly, cultural heritage experts have used digital media to enable heritage-based cultural learning. Such work entails understanding and creatively exploiting the expressive potential of the digital medium. As the Themescaping Virtual Collections research project found, museum educators and teachers espoused the potential of virtual reality and augmented reality for creating immersive experiences to achieve learning objectives related to heritage collections. Three-dimensional models of objects, for example, permitted students to more completely explore the objects. Three-dimensional environments, similarly, help to contextualize cultural heritage objects and suggest spatial relations between objects. Cameron and Robinson (2007) note that the educators readily perceived the technique's relevance to youth education. Children need to be able to visually explore connections between objects, as well as their contexts. Teachers commented on the relative shortcomings of text-based learning tools in favor of engaging youth in immersive experiences (Cameron and Robinson 2007).

Key to this pedagogical approach is replacing text with experience-based, affectively interactive, immersive digital media. Creating these virtual heritage environments, however, necessitates grappling with the dual challenges of creating an intriguing illusion into which the audience will be enticed to enter and stay, and successfully delivering accurate cultural information and conveying fact-based lessons. According to Kenderdine (2007), virtual heritage learning projects must negotiate "the traditional panoramic strategies used in creating spaces of immersion and illusion—in conjunction with [their] pedagogical functions. The provocative tension that exists for virtual heritage as a tool for scientific and cultural visualizations resonates between the scientific requirement to reproduce rational material reality, and those 'sensations' of the 'Electronic Baroque' that intrigue visitors to the space" (323).

The spatial trend of much cultural heritage work affects the nature of the audience's experience with the data in profound ways. Cameron and Robinson (2007) note that digital media tend to produce increased emphasis on action and mental engagement. The spatial presentation facilitates new ways to present and interact with data—moving audience engagement from that of reading text to exploration of user-centered interpretive environments.

As we discuss in the next section, cultural heritage practitioners have looked to video games as models for constructing navigable and interactive environments to facilitate cultural learning. To understand the potential application to cultural heritage, however, a brief review of spatial storytelling in video games is necessary.

Spatial Storytelling in Video Games

As video game theorists point out, storytelling in video games is largely a spatial affair. The narrative primarily unfolds through traversal of the game environment and by providing opportunities for the player to interact with features and figures of the game world. As Fuller and Jenkins (2004) argue, many stories can be understood as travel narratives (Jenkins 2004), based on the human desire to explore space. Sustained attention to plot and character emerged slowly in this kind of storytelling—based on travel writing—which is so tied up with exploration of spaces.

The adaptation of plot-centered contemporary films into spatial narratives can be seen as a continuation of a long history of travel writing, science fiction, and fantasy writing dedicated to the exploration and mastery of unknown spaces. In this kind of story, it is space rather than plot that serves as the central organizing principle. In games, one can act within and transform these spaces (Fuller and Jenkins 1995).

Games present worlds and allow movement between levels in order to experience new spectacles. The goal of the game storyteller is to construct multiple ways to interact with compelling spaces. Nintendo games, for example, present some fascinating spaces that players cannot wait to access—while we are ostensibly on the quest to save Princess Toadstool, we are also really hoping to just get to the next level so we can experience the spectacle that will be revealed to us as a reward. In much game storytelling, characters play a relatively minimal role; their characteristics may be mainly built around capabilities for action, like supernatural strength or fighting ability. Some games in fact draw on characters that are taken from other media (such as the *Law and Order* computer games based on the television show or the Nancy Drew mystery games based on the children's book character). Use of such characters allows the games to evoke rather than to fully develop the characters. In addition, plot may become primarily atmosphere for the player to explore. This is especially evident in the game adaptations of films or television series—moments in the narrative become places in the player's itinerary, preserved as a series of worlds to be traversed in order to pursue goals. In this sense narrative points become places to be explored (Fuller and Jenkins 1995; Jenkins 2004).

For theorist Michel de Certeau (1994), narrative transforms places into spaces. In this place/space distinction, places can be understood as potential sites for narrative action, while spaces are places that have been acted upon (explored). Places exist but do not "matter"; they become meaningful as they interact with story agents. In this sense, spaces serve as locations for narrative events. Distinctions can also be usefully drawn between maps and tours. In this conception, maps are abstract representations of spatial relations that document places; tours, on the other hand, describe movements through spaces—from the perspective of the traveler. In this sense, tours depict movements and possible effects of movements (for example, a door may serve as a threshold between two rooms, rather than just being an element of a building). Spaces in a game story do not exist entirely separately from the audience's goals and desires; they are linked not only to actions but also to goals. Players must enter unfamiliar spaces, confronting conflict, in order to master the game (Fuller and Jenkins 1995).

De Certeau (1994) also discusses the importance of frontiers, which can be understood as functioning to separate the known from the unknown (think of the phrase "Space, the final frontier"). This idea of the frontier as the line that separates the known from the unknown may involve having the player face dangerous beings or fight for control of the story space along this frontier. The question becomes one of possession, or determining who controls a given space. It is important to remember that the narrative space of the game is not necessarily visible all at once; rather, the frontier line may be presented through the division of the story's space into a succession of screens. Games often have what are called "guideposts," which establish movement through space and mastery or control over it. Generally, increased understanding of the geography of the world contained within a game allows the player to rapidly come back to the same space and progress further into the frontier (Fuller and Jenkins 1995).

Scholars such as Flynn (2007) have suggested that virtual heritage practitioners look into video games for models of interactivity and spatiality for cultural heritage work. Flynn mentions games such as EverQuest, Ultima Online, Civilization, and Grand Theft Auto, all of which provide models of user-driven navigation and interactive spatial landscapes. The digital media consumer, Flynn notes, becomes less a passive receiver of knowledge than an active participant; rather than amassing facts, the primary activity is that of immersion, and instead of static structure, there is dynamic agency.

The integration of choice, Flynn (2007) points out, offers players the opportunity to undertake tasks relevant to their knowledge level, enables exploration leading to discovery, and leads to a sense of "being there." An early example is the virtual Florida Everglades Project (1998), based on the Unreal game engine. Using this game engine enabled creators to create a sense of "being there" through such techniques as 3-D visualization. Flynn notes that in so doing, the creators were after more than authentic representation; rather, they attempted to create a simulation of organic systems.

Flynn also suggests that digital cultural heritage practitioners look to commercial video games as models for providing a range of types of spatial experiences for the player:

> These modes of spatiality contribute to game-play through such strategies as constraint and concealment, challenging the player to negotiate terrain to access objects, meet avatars, find portals, and do battle . . . One aspect that makes games so interesting is that the environment—the roads, bridges, paths, and doorways—cannot be perceived as a whole all at once by the player. Building up knowledge requires commitment to a series of spectorial voyages—an extensive exploration of terrain through panoramas, cartographic maps, isometric diagrams, abstract expressionist planes, and geometric landscapes. Through these sets of spatial negotiations, players become involved in the sequential unfolding of a record of signposts and metaphors embedded in the landscape. (355)

From a phenomenological standpoint, space is what surrounds the body and results from a particular spatial situation. This is precisely what game designers attempt to create—space as enabled by bodily movement, allowing players to understand and immerse themselves within it. Flynn (2007) offers the example of Grand Theft Auto as a game in which players create their spatial domain through real-time spatial acts.

Rather than being primarily revealed through devices like narration, then, space is revealed to the player during the course of playing the game. Thus, the spaces in the computer game exist before and after their role in the story. Such ideas allow the cultural heritage expert to move beyond a directional and limited space to an embodied mode of invoking the past, which in turn enables embodied subjectivity. As ethnographers and others explore the structure and meaning of virtual worlds and the virtually human, new opportunities emerge for a form of digital cultural representation that simulates cultural ideas, values, and experience. The next chapter presents a cultural heritage computer game project at UCF that provides opportunities for cultural learning through computer game and interactive story design.

CHAPTER 6

Cultural Heritage Video Game Design

Evidence of the increasing scholarly attention to video games is evident. Recent work has proliferated at the intersection of games and culture in areas including online gaming culture (Morris 2004; Taylor 2006), the popular culture and presence of archetypes in games (Berger 2002; Tews 2001), and identity issues in games (Consalvo 2003; Taylor and Kolko 2003). In this chapter we focus not on the study of but on the production of a computer game project in order to explore how an ethnographic perspective—which has always, as Boellstorff (2008) reminds us, been virtual in a sense—can be embedded in a medium that focuses on action and mental engagement (Cameron and Robinson 2007).

Introduction to the Project

The Turkey Maiden Educational Computer Game (J), directed by Underberg (2008), is based on a Spanish folktale collected in 1930s Ybor City, Florida, by folklorist Ralph Steele Boggs. Using the narrative structure of the folktale as the basic game story outline, a group of students (graduate and undergraduate) under the direction of Underberg developed an educational computer game mod (a modification to a commercial video game) that set the game story in the time and place from which the story was collected: Depression-era Ybor City, Florida. They accomplished this through using the toolset included with the Never-Winter Nights game—"hakpaks," or custom content created by game fans for other game fans—and through creating original content (**K**).

"The Turkey Maiden" is a folktale that was published as "La Pavera" in *Southern Folklore Quarterly* in 1938 (Boggs 1938); it was translated into English by Maria Redmon for publication in Kristin Congdon's collection *Uncle Monday and Other Florida Tales* (Congdon 2002). The setting of the game—Depression-era Ybor City—facilitates exploration of specific aspects of the area's history and culture.

Ybor City's history is intimately tied to the area's cigar industry and the cultural traditions of the Cuban, Spanish, and Italian immigrants who lived and worked there. Cigar makers from Cuba, from Key West, Florida, and other parts of the United States came to Ybor City to establish their factories. The area became famous for its Cuban cigars, and was called the Cigar Capital of the World.

To create appropriate game-related tasks and quests, Underberg explored Federal Writers' Project Works Progress Administration (WPA) documentation related to Ybor City. These materials, including folktales, journalistic observations of daily life, and so on, provided a rich body of information related to customs and historical events from which to draw in the development of the game.

In the game mod, the main points of the plot remained the same; the challenge was to link the plot points to sites on the player's path. The folktale begins with Rosa, the heroine, unhappily living at home with her widowed father, who has married a new wife with two daughters of her own. Rosa decides to leave home because of the suffering she experiences at home, but not before her kindly father gives her a magic gift of three nuts, which he instructs her to open when she needs help. One day in the forest, she finds herself chased by men, and she opens the first of her magical nuts; it contains a dress made of wood, which serves to hide her from her would-be attackers. Later, Rosa becomes cold and hungry, and she opens a second nut, from which springs a magical dwarf who provides her with food and warmth. Eventually the heroine makes her way to a palace, where she takes up employment as a turkey herder (hence the story's title). Still dressed in her wooden dress, she is spotted one day by the prince, who laughs at her appearance. She becomes sad, and the dwarf proposes a cure: to create a dress from flowers and to dance (because it's springtime). The prince mistakes her for a fairy and falls in love with her. The prince then falls ill, and no one, it seems, can cure him. After multiple attempts, Rosa is finally able to enter the palace, and, once inside, opens the third nut, to reveal a beautiful dress. She puts it on, the prince sees her, is cured, and they get married (Boggs 1938; Congdon 2002).

Adapting a linear folktale into a digital game necessitated thinking of the story as progressing along specific plot points that could be linked to specific environments in a way that would resonate with the characterization of digital cultural heritage as a form of tourism (Kenderdine 2007). As Fuller and Jenkins (1995) and Jenkins (2004) point out, the adaptation of stories from linear to interactive narrative involves transforming narrative elements into sites on a player's path. To facilitate this, spaces related to Ybor City history and culture that could be explored at particular plot points were identified, with the aim of conveying a sense of "being there" and the simulation of a world (Flynn 2007). These included the *casita*, or house, where Rosa begins her journey; the woods outside the house, where she flees from the pursuing men; and downtown Ybor City, where she encounters the prince.

While playing the game, players navigate from space to space in a way that correlates to the plot progression of the folktale, so that quests must be completed within one environment before the player can successfully move through the next. Such immersion and user agency transform the student from a passive to an active participant (Flynn 2007). For example, the player has to figure out how to help Rosa's father locate a particular story to read to the cigar factory workers before he gives her the gift she will need on her journey. Such a design allows players to simulate being persecuted, pursued, ridiculed, and loved, much as the heroine experiences in the folktale.

The Turkey Maiden game was designed to convey specific lessons about Ybor City history and culture, each of which is reinforced by the game curriculum, which students complete after playing the game. The game outline and curriculum are based on a number of historical works on Ybor City (Bane and Moore 1981; Brynan 1939; Dunn 1972; Ingalls and Perez 2003; Mormino and Pizzo 1983). Giving those works an interpretive frame allows students to move beyond facts to abstract ideas (Squire in press). A challenge, as Kenderdine (2007) argues, is to balance the creation of an engaging illusion with accurately conveyed facts.

Cultural Heritage Video Game Design: The Turkey Maiden Game Outline

The rationale for design followed in this game outline (L) resonates with Flynn's (2007) admonition to create virtual spaces with room for emotions and thoughts as well as three-dimensional representations of physical places. These aspects of belief, custom, and ideology were embedded in a narrative that unfolds through traversal of space and interaction with objects, avatars, and places (Fuller and Jenkins 2004; Jenkins 1995).

The first lesson in the game is designed to expose students to the historic role of the *lector* (reader) in the cigar factories. Readers played an important role in Ybor City culture, entertaining and informing cigar factory workers before the days of the widespread availability of radio. The first task that Rosa must complete is to leave the house where she is being mistreated by her stepmother and stepsisters. To receive the magical nuts from her father, Rosa must find a particular folktale for her father to read at the factory the next day, where he works as a *lector* (reader). This becomes a lesson in Ybor City folklore, history, and the role of the press in the area, as well as an opportunity to have students explore the very materials the readers may have read to the workers.

The second lesson in the Turkey Maiden game concerns the cigar industry trade itself, including the role of women in it. Rosa's second task is to open the nut to escape danger. She cannot open the nut without finding something hard with which to crack it. She meets a female cigar roller who has a special knife (*chaveta*) used to cut the wrapper leaf, but the worker will not help Rosa until she finds her missing tobacco leaves. This becomes a lesson in the leaves of the Vuelto Abajo region of Cuba and the importance of the cigar-rolling industry in Ybor City.

The third lesson involves teaching students about the importance of immigrant mutual aid societies. Rosa's third task is to open the second nut in order to gain food and warmth. At this point a helper dwarf appears; he will not lead her to the site of food and warmth until she can correctly identify the Centro Asturiano (a Spanish cultural center) for him, using historical information she must find in the game. This becomes a lesson in the role of cultural centers in Ybor City.

The fourth lesson explores the role of dance and festivities in Depression-era Ybor City culture. This lesson relates to the plot point in the folktale where Rosa feels sad after the prince laughs at her wooden dress. For this task, Rosa must find a Spanish *jota* dancer (a dancer from the Asturias region in Spain) in order to learn the dance and cheer herself up; the prince is reimagined as the son of the cigar factory owner. This situation presents an opportunity for the player to interact with different dancers in Ybor City and discover through conversation with nonplayable characters (NPCs) how folk dances are similar to and different from each other. This becomes a lesson about traditional dances, as Rosa must interact with other types of dancers to identify the correct dance (see Ray 2004 for a discussion of integrating backstory and exposition into game design).

Finally, students are introduced to the importance of José Martí for Ybor City and the struggle for Cuban independence. For this lesson, Rosa faces the challenge of getting into the "palace," reimagined for the game as the home of "El Rey," the owner of the cigar factory, to save El Rey's son, who has fallen ill with a sickness of the heart. Rosa must first get past the man who guards the entrance to the home, which is next to the factory. The guard, a native of Cuba, will not let her in until she can tell him the story of José Martí, the great revolutionary leader who led the cause for Cuban independence. Conversations are key to enabling the player to complete tasks and learn about Ybor City culture and history. Rosa appeals to the man's fatherly side, asking him if he has children. He replies that he does, in fact, have kids, who have been named after the "great José Martí." Rosa cannot tell him who Martí is, and he demands that she learn this important piece of local history before he will let her enter. Rosa (and the player) must peruse archival documents and converse with other NPCs to piece together the story of Martí.

Creating Navigable Virtual Environments Based on Cultural and Historical Materials

As we discussed in the previous chapter, computer game storytelling has traditionally been characterized as primarily spatial. In this sense, storytelling occurs through exploration of an environment and by allowing the player to interact with the objects and NPCs within it—thus transforming "places" into "spaces" imbued with meaning (Fuller and Jenkins 1995; Jenkins 2004). Because the Turkey Maiden mod is based on a European folktale, it is useful to begin by considering the style of the folktale and its representation of space. Max Lüthi's (1976) formalist study of the folktale reveals its world to be fundamentally linear and two-dimensional. The tale exhibits a basic polarized structure— victory versus defeat, reward versus punishment, and is characterized by a general lack of description. In addition, objects in the folktale are typically presented as fixed and immutable. Much is left to the imagination of the audience.

Alfred Messerli (2005), drawing on Lüthi, examines the representation of space in European folktales, focusing on economy in spatial organization, discontinuity in order of perception of space, and the significance of narrative perspective. Central to the notion of economy in spatial representation is the ability of the listener or reader to provide a form of completion to the spatial information so sparsely narrated in the traditional tale. We see this in the use of acoustic signals (knocking at the door, for example) that function to suggest movement through space. Rather than being revealed through narration—and only when absolutely necessary—computer game space is revealed to the player in the course of gameplay. These spaces exist before, and after, their direct role in the action of the linear narrative.

The capacity for computer games to provide an expansive and potentially complex spatial environment formed the rationale behind the designers' decision to situate the game-story of "The Turkey Maiden" in the very space and time from which the tale was originally collected, 1930s Ybor City. Spaces for which models were developed using 3-D software were chosen for their historical and cultural significance to Ybor City as well as their ability to stand in for fairy-tale world correlates: the *casita*, or cigar worker's home, doubles as the site of the initial action in the tale before the heroine embarks on her main adventure; the Centro Asturiano (a mutual aid society for Spanish immigrants) is used as the space of food and warmth provided by a helper figure in the tale; and the cigar factory and the large *casita* next door double as the palace in the game where the "prince" (or the son of El Rey, the cigar factory owner) and the factory owner live and oversee their "empire."

Thus, the game follows the plot of "The Turkey Maiden" while at the same time providing opportunities to interact with primary source materials in a way that advances the game. For example, in the *casita* Rosa's father, a *lector* or reader in the cigar factory, has a collection of written works. These include collections of folktales, riddles, and other aspects of Spanish and Cuban traditional culture documented by the WPA during the Depression. To be able to receive the gift of nuts from her father and thus leave the *casita* space to seek her fortune, Rosa (and the player) must successfully peruse these materials to find the answer to a specific question posed by her father. In this way, primary materials are embedded in the game environment in a way that resonates with McGregor's (2007) notion of codified space, in which the game environment encodes information and becomes itself a kind of interface.

In developing the game and curriculum for this project, then, principles of video game design were combined with cultural heritage research and practice to create a cultural learning experience for young people. The goal of such a project is to provide middle and high school students with an educational computer game and follow-up lessons that allow them to learn about local Florida history and culture.

Thus far in this book we have explored digital ethnography as a tool for cultural expression, as an aid to anthropological analysis, and as a medium for cultural heritage learning. In the conclusion we offer some final thoughts on how these three aspects of digital ethnography interrelate and discuss roles for new media in the areas of critical and narrative anthropology.

Conclusion: Narratives and Critical Anthropology: Roles for New Media

Berta, an eight-year-old girl, is lying on the grass on her back in the Peruvian *puna* (high plateau), looking up at the sky. Seeing a condor fly overhead, Berta says:

> Seeing the condor flying overhead makes me feel so safe, like I'm being watched over. But I'm lonely, and wish I had a play-mate to play with. The stories they tell, though, like "The Condor Seeks a Wife," seem kind of silly to me, and I don't know why they keep telling the same fanciful tales over and over in my pueblo. Why should I listen to these stories? How could they possibly help me in my daily life? I should probably set aside these "silly" fantasies and do something useful, like help my mother spin and weave to prepare goods for the *trueque* (barter market).

Berta stands up and begins walking in the direction of her house down the hill. A group of condors is perched on a hillside. They are hovering around what appears to be a dead cow. The condors turn their heads toward Berta.

She hears their plea: "Help us divide up our offering to our mountain god."

"Could that be the condors?" Berta exclaims, surprised. "Condors don't talk; in fact, they don't have a voice box at all to make any sounds."

As if in response, the condors reply in unison: "Berta, help us."

"Wait," says Berta. "I've heard this before. It's a tale my mother used to tell me called 'The She-Calf.' Should I help the condors or not? Who can help me?" she asks, sitting down by the side of the running stream. As if in response to her query, the water explains: "You know, the Inca believed that the Apu Ilapi's (rain god) shadow was located in the Milky Way, where he drew the water that poured down to earth as rain. The rain flows into the rivers, which irrigate the land, so all the living things can eat. It was believed to later return to the sky in a cycle that was repeated. You see, we have to help each other. We call it *ayni*, reciprocity, and it's a very important value for us. You should always seek to give, whether it be to your family or neighbor, or to the Earth, or to the universe itself. That's how everything stays in balance."

Shaking her head in disbelief, but carrying the words she's heard in her head, Berta walks across the *puna* and approaches a man walking in the field who is carrying a bundle in his arms.

"What are you doing?" Berta asks. "And why?"

The man replies: "In our village, people work on projects on each other's land so that we benefit from each other's help. For example, I'm up here helping with my cousin's *chacra* (farm), while my uncle is helping our neighbor on his farm. You see, we have to help each other. We call it *ayni*, reciprocity, and it's a very important value for us. You should always seek to give, whether it be to your family or neighbor, or to the Earth. That's how everything stays in balance."

Berta is starting to see a pattern, but she decides to talk to her aunt, who is shearing sheep.

"Aunt," Berta asks, "Why are you doing that?"

Her aunt replies: "I'm shearing this sheep so we can make weavings. I can't make the beautiful weavings, though, without the brightly colored wool. So I trade my wool for dye with the woman down the hill [the woman with the pink dye in her pot below], and then I can have the colored wool I need. It's called *trueque*, barter or exchange, and it's how we get what we need and give others what they need. You see, we have to help each other.

We call it *ayni*, reciprocity, and it's a very important value for us. You should always seek to give, whether it be to your family or neighbor, or to the Earth. That's how everything stays in balance."

Berta nods and gives her aunt a hug. "I think I understand now," she says, walking back toward the condors. "Helping the condors divide up their offering would be in keeping with the value of *ayni* that the river, the man in the field, and my aunt have been talking about."

Berta continues her virtual walk-through of an animated, interactive story cloth based on the work of Andean artist Flora Zárate, who does *arpillera* (appliqué art). Berta—and the student interactor—will be invited to ask broad questions such as these: How are we connected to other people, to things, and to the earth? To what am I responsible in this world? Does the environment have moral standing?

Berta's narrative is based on Virtual Taller, a project under development (Underberg, J. Michael Moshell, and James Mason) that has the aim of building a pilot interactive and immersive story experience based on Peruvian folklore and cultural heritage. Specifically, the project is based on the work of Peruvian *arpillera* (appliqué) artist Flora Zárate, whose three-dimensional "story cloths" narrate cultural stories both of people from her native Peru and of immigrants in the United States. Cultural narratives such as folktales, myths, and personal experience stories are woven into the interactive story experience, which allows the audience to learn about Hispanic heritage while at the same time making connections with their own community heritage.

Taking a cue from earlier work at the intersection of literary, visual, and hypermedia anthropology, hypertext theory, and cultural heritage studies, the interactive story script is based on key themes in Andean mythology, including the idea of people as linked to the land. Another key theme is the idea of power and wealth being expressed through cooperative labor. In addition to identifying key themes in Andean mythology, we considered how elements of mythic thinking and Andean worldview that figure in

Quechua folktales—such as the presence of religious syncretism, the relation between time and space in Andean thought, and the conception of gender complementarity and dependence—could be integrated into the design of the interactive experience in an age-appropriate way. These recurring themes in Andean thought and narrative were then identified in the *arpilleras* themselves, illustrated by, for example, the presence of the important Andean symbol of the condor inhabiting the realm of the upper world and the presence of male-female pairs throughout the artwork.

Creation of this augmented reality experience (involving projected images, animation, a physical *arpillera*, and immersive sound) requires developing certain "building blocks" of digital ethnographic storytelling, including an introduction that establishes the setting and delivers necessary exposition; places or important points in the setting as they relate to characters and objects; characters, including their names, roles, and corresponding knowledge and tasks; objects, including their potential uses; and conversations, including the accompanying interface (input, output, and visualizations). Throughout the interactive experience, Berta (the main character—and, by extension, the interactor) will have to make choices that relate to Andean culture, including understanding and demonstrating the importance of reciprocity (translated into age-appropriate terms as "you have to give in order to receive").

Toward Digital Ethnography

The goal of this book has been to provide readers with a theoretical and practice-oriented overview of the ways in which the disciplines of anthropology and digital media can be combined in order to help artists, communities, and anthropologists express new insights into culture. To accomplish this aim, we have focused on three avenues through which digital media and anthropology can usefully complement each other in digital ethnography: (1) employing digital media as an expressive tool for creative cultural representations; (2) using digital media as a tool for anthropological research and analysis; and (3) utilizing digital media to enable heritage-based education.

The book seeks to do this by drawing on key texts in the emerging field of digital anthropology and combining close reading of scholarly literature with analysis and practice for real-world applied projects. We first located the discourses of anthropology and digital media within larger conversations about interdisciplinarity and the changing roles of the "expert" in the new technological landscape. Then, in Chapters 1 and 2, we considered how digital media can be used as an expressive tool to create cultural representations, examining efforts to integrate insights from literary and visual ethnography with new media theory and production. This work is inspired by such pioneers as Zora Neale Hurston (in literary ethnography), Karl Heider (in visual anthropology), and Sarah Pink (in the emerging field of sensory ethnography), and involves adapting ethnographic materials using ideas from literary and multimedia storytelling. An important area of consideration in this field of study is that of collaborative design with source communities, which, after all, provide the ethnographic data from which these representations originate (see, for example, the participatory design model as outlined by Watkins 2007), and increasingly and rightfully claim a place at the table, oftentimes in the lead, of interpreting their communities as part of the multivocality of interpretation.

Later in the book, in Chapters 3 and 4, we explored how digital media has been used as a tool for anthropological analysis. Anthropologists have grappled with (and sometimes initially missed) the potential of recent computer technology developments to augment their research aims. Whether in the realm of using computer tools for data analysis, using hypertext itself as a distribution and communication medium for scholarship, or contributing to culturally oriented database design, anthropologists are finding digital media increasingly useful in their research.

Insights from previous and ongoing work with Rudy McDaniel in the areas of personal experience narratives, game-based learn-

PeruDigital cultural consultants Norma Ledesma (left) and Flora Zárate (right). Courtesy: Natalie M. Underberg.

ing in the humanities, and Puerto Rican oral history and newspaper accounts are being integrated into the expansion of the PeruDigital project (in collaboration with former graduate student Patricia Abón). This involves designing and developing state-of-the-art, innovative ways to share educational material as a free-content web-based rich multimedia encyclopedia based on anonymous and non-anonymous contributions. The goals are to increase access to the ethnographic data contained in PeruDigital and to provide a way for the general public to contribute information and knowledge to further enrich the collections. As scholars and users know, Web 2.0 includes many types of software that allow users to interact and share information. Conceived of as a web-based encyclopedia, it will combine features from existing applications such as Flickr, Wikipedia, and YouTube, which will allow users to show their input and knowledge through tags and comments. In addition to implementing a search engine, the project will allow users to create an account that carries with it the ability to add tags (allowing for user-generated information classification), add comments, and upload content. In particular, Flickr Commons, Wikimedia Commons, and Wikiversity will be integrated into the project design.

Chapters 5 and 6 explored the potential of virtual heritage and computer game studies for designing heritage-based cultural learning experiences. In developing educational media based on cultural heritage materials, scholars and practitioners need to balance the demands of ethnographic accuracy with an understanding of new media's ability to simulate cultural ideas and processes.

The game-based cultural learning in digital heritage that Underberg explored in the Turkey Maiden Educational Computer Game is the inspiration for an expansion of the Peru-Digital project into a project entitled Mobile Folk (in collaboration with human-computer interaction specialist Si-Jung "Jun" Kim). Grounded in the web-based cultural learning experience of the PeruDigital project, the Mobile Folk digital ethnography project will empower participants from diverse cultural heritages to learn about and create cultural learning modules using handheld mobile devices. By taking the experience out of the website and placing it into users' hands and the social spaces in which they live, participants will be able to create their own interactive experiences based on folklore fieldwork in their home communities. As part of the creation of these interactive modules, users will have the opportunity to adopt one of three roles in relation to experiencing expressive culture (organizer/sponsor, performer/artist, or ethnographer/folklorist), and use this experience to learn about not only the performance and consumption of, but also the production of, folklore and cultural heritage. As a result, participants will be able to create their own interactive experiences based on folklore fieldwork in their home communities and share them with the public through mobile technologies.

Such work, of necessity, raises important questions surrounding how "interventionist" or "activist" anthropologists should be in not only using but also potentially developing such technologies. Whether and how digital technologies enable the process of democratizing information (Jenkins and Thorburn 2004; Pfaffenberger 1990), serve to widen the "digital divide" (Wresch 1996, among others), or something more ambiguous and complex (see the excellent volume from the Social Science Research Council edited by Joe Karaganis 2007, for example) is a question anthropologists are particularly well suited to examine. This is due, we argue, not only to their skill in ethnographic research within bounded "cultures" (well understood and equally well appropriated by adjacent fields), but also to their tradition of balancing micro- with macro-level fields of analysis (so that, for example, what happens in the "lab" is understood as inexorably linked to wider flows of information, communication, and power).

We hope this book contributes to this project as ethnographers continue to struggle to articulate their particular role and unique contributions in the new media environment of digital ethnography. Time will tell how this approach develops in the future.

Guide to Web-Based Materials

These web-based materials are denoted in the text by boldface letters (e.g., **A**). The links are current as of this writing.

A: A guide for working with oral history narrators to co-create digital stories. Available at http://www.svad.ucf.edu/digitalethnography/research.html (click on link to Oral History Exhibition Curriculum).

B: The PeruDigital project website splash page. Available at http://www.perudigital.org.

C: The original PeruDigital design document from the first phase of development. Available at http://digitalethnography.dm.ucf.edu/pv/research.html (click on the box that reads "Introductory Presentation," toward the right-hand side of the screen).

D: The original PeruDigital pilot project. Available at http://digitalethnography.dm.ucf.edu/pv/home.html.

E: A curriculum developed by Underberg and Jo Anne Adams based on their Scholarship of Teaching and Learning (SoTL) project to redesign PeruDigital in collaboration with digital media students. Available at http://www.svad.ucf.edu/digitalethnography/research.html (click on link to PeruDigital curriculum).

F: The PeruDigital Lima, Peru, plaza interactive environment. Available at http://digitalethnography.dm.ucf.edu/pv/PlazaFrancia.htm.

G: The PeruDigital Piura, Peru, interactive environment. Available at http://digitalethnography.dm.ucf.edu/pv/Piura1.html.

H: The PeruDigital website curriculum, based on the perspectives of festival sponsor, performer, and ethnographer. Available at http://digitalethnography.dm.ucf.edu/pv/curriculum.html (click on "the performer," "the sponsor," or "the ethnographer").

I: Sample digital stories from the Puerto Ricans in the Central Florida

oral history project. Available at http://www.digitalethnography.dm.ucf
.edu/pr/community.html.

J: The UCF Digital Ethnography Lab Turkey Maiden project website.
Available at http://www.digitalethnography.dm.ucf.edu/turkeymaiden
.html.

K: The Turkey Maiden curriculum for the Directed Research game design course. Available at http://www.svad.ucf.edu/digitalethnography
/research.html (click on link to Turkey Maiden curriculum).

L: The Turkey Maiden game outline. Available at http://www.digital
ethnography.dm.ucf.edu/tmgameoutline.html.

Glossary

Apache Apache is a widely used open-source database server. It was developed by a number of volunteers and first released in 1995.

augmented reality Augmented reality combines real-world and computer-generated data. In augmented reality, a physical environment is augmented by computer-generated images and sensory input.

avatar An avatar is a computer-generated three-dimensional image representing someone in a virtual environment. It may be a two-dimensional image or a moving three-dimensional figure.

blog Short for "web log" or "weblog," a blog originally was a type of online diary in the form of a website owned and created by an individual; blogs have become increasingly commercialized for business.

cyberculture Cyberculture refers to the distinctive identity formations and community constructions enabled by digitally networked technologies.

cyberspace Cyberspace is a nonphysical environment that enables individuals to interact with other individuals or with sets of information or entertainment via digital connections.

digital asset A digital asset is content or media that has been formatted into a binary source. It may include text, graphics, video, audio, animation, and so on, and is generally conceived of as owned by an individual or organizational entity.

digital media Digital media is any type of electronic media that is based on binary code. Examples include the web, video games, digital audio or video, and artwork created using computer software.

digitization Digitization is the process of converting images, sound, or data into digital form. When text is digitized, the image of the text may be scanned and then converted into digital text via optical character recognition (OCR). Digitization makes archived materials easier to store and more accessible. Once digitized, text documents can be searched by keywords.

disambiguation In language, one word can have more than one meaning. Through disambiguation, a program will search the text surrounding an ambiguous word for contextual clues.

document type definition (DTD) A document type definition defines the structure—the elements and attributes—of a markup language such as XML, HTML, or XHTML. The DTD interpretation may be strict or transitional.

Dreamweaver Dreamweaver is a software program, created by Macromedia and now owned by Adobe, that enables designers with no knowledge of programming to create interactive websites. Dreamweaver allows the web page to be edited visually.

Drupal Drupal is an open-source content management program used to build websites.

extensible markup language Extensible markup language (XML) is a metadata, or descriptive data, classification system. It is a simplified version of SGML and is designed to structure, transport, and store data.

Facebook Facebook is a popular social networking website that allows users to create personal profiles and to communicate with others through their profile page.

Flash Flash is a program developed by Macromedia and now owned by the Adobe corporation that is used to create and deliver multimedia presentations, websites, and animations.

Flickr Flickr is a photo-sharing website that lets users upload and share photographs.

game mod A game mod is a modification of an off-the-shelf commercial game. Mods can be made by members of the general public, allowing them to add to or change aspects of an existing game. For example, they may add new items, models, or music.

hypermedia Hypermedia refers to digital graphics, audio, or video that is linked to related objects, web pages, or media.

hypertext Hypertext is the nonlinear or multilinear presentation of information in networked form, which enables multiple ways to read the information, along with the increased potential for participation by audiences and an accompanying redefinition of the roles of author, audience, and text.

hypertext markup language (HTML) HTML is a type of markup language that provides instructions to the web browser on how a page should look and work.

hypertext preprocessor (PHP) PHP is a freely available scripting language and interpreter.

iMovie iMovie is a movie-editing software application, owned by Apple, that makes it possible for users to create and edit movies from various types of sources.

keyword analysis A keyword analysis tool uses an algorithm to report on frequency of keywords used in searches. The data generated from the analysis will help web designers include keywords that will attract a higher volume of visitors.

light detection and ranging (LIDAR) LIDAR uses lasers to determine the distance between objects. This technology is used to create 3-D topographical maps, atmospheric imaging, and geographical surveys.

metatag A metatag is a type of tag that contains information about a web page but is not visible in the web browser. It can be used to store information such as descriptions or keywords. This information can then be located by a search engine.

nonplayable characters (NPCs) In computer games, NPCs are computer-controlled characters that cannot be used by the player.

online portal An online portal (or web portal) is a website through which the user can browse for other websites. Portals can be broad or specialized.

open-source technologies Open-source technologies are free to the public and are generally part of a production practice that encourages making software widely available without cost.

optical character recognition (OCR) OCR converts digital images of scanned text into actual text. The OCR document can be stored more conveniently and accessed through keyword searches.

parse To parse is to break down text or computer code into manageable, functional components and check code for correct syntax.

Photoshop Photoshop is an Adobe software program for editing digital photos and creating digital images.

protoype A prototype is an original instance of an object, serving as a standard for future objects in that category.

relational database A relational database enables users to search records by more than one field. Records are stored not in one database, but in a group of databases that are linked to each other with a series of ID keys.

role-playing games Role-playing games stress social interaction and collaboration. During a role-playing game, players assume different roles and base their actions upon a system of rules outlined by the game. Varieties of role-playing games include "pen-and-paper" forms, such as Dungeons and Dragons, Live Action Role-Playing, and single and multi-user computer video games such as Multi-User Dungeons.

search engine A search engine is a software application that uses algorithms to retrieve a list of results (web pages) based upon keywords that a user submits. Frequently used search engines include Google, Yahoo, and Bing, and most large websites include a search engine.

semantic web A semantic web is a constellation of data and a collection of technologies that enable computers to interpret data and process it without human direction.

server-side scripting language Server-side scripting is used to create dynamic web pages by running scripts on the web server—as opposed to the user's browser—so that the user can interface with a database and receive responses based on the user's input.

standard generalized markup language (SGML) SGML is the parent language of HTML. It is a system of defining markup languages that describe a document's structure and attributes.

structural linkage Structural linkages (hyperlinks) are items (text, media, navigation bars) that allow the user to navigate via mouse click to a related document or portion of a document.

text encoding initiative (TEI) TEI is a consortium that develops and maintains standards for representation of text in digital form and specifications for encoding machine-readable texts that are used by libraries and museums and in the humanities.

toolset A toolset is a set of software tools that enables a game mod user to create his or her own custom content for a computer game. Toolsets may include tools for building a virtual environment (e.g., terrain, a dungeon, furniture, lighting), plots, scripts, and conversations. Toolsets allow users to create their own stories.

Twitter Twitter is an online network for sharing information in text messages of 140 characters or fewer.

virtual reality Virtual reality is the computer simulation of a three-dimensional space with which the audience can interact.

virtual world A virtual world is a nonphysical, digitally created environment with which one or more users or players can interact.

visualization systems Visualization systems enable data visualization, which is a method of communicating information through graphic means.

Web 2.0 Web 2.0 is a loosely defined intersection of web application features that not only delivers static images and text but also facilitates user interactivity (social networking, tagging, collaborative authoring, media distribution, keyword searches, and more).

web portal A web portal (or online portal) is a website through which the user can browse for other websites. Portals can be broad or specialized.

wiki A wiki is a website with server software that lets users both create and edit content on web pages, using a web browser. Wiki comes from the Hawaiian word for "quick."

XML tag   XML, like HTML and SGML, requires tags—the identifiers that appear between angled brackets. Tags are keywords used to classify content. In XML (as opposed to HTML), tags must be created by the user.

YouTube   YouTube is an online video-sharing site. It allows users to upload short videos for others to view.

References Cited

Agar, Michael (1983). Microcomputers as Field Tools. *Computers and the Humanities* 17(1): 19–26.

Allen, Catherine J. (2002). *The Hold Life Has: Coca and Cultural Identity in an Andean Community*. Washington, DC: Smithsonian Institution Press.

Arguedas, José María. (2002). *Deep Rivers*. Long Grove, IL: Waveland Press.

———. (1958). Notas elementales sobre el arte popular religioso y la cultura mestiza de Huamanga. *Revista del Museo Nacional* 27: 140–194.

Asad, Talal. (1986). The Concept of Cultural Translation in British Social Anthropology. In J. Clifford and G. E. Marcus, eds., *Writing Culture: The Poetics and Politics of Ethnography*. Berkeley: University of California Press: 141–164.

Babb, Florence E. (1998). *Between Field and Cooking Pot: The Political Economy of Marketwomen in Peru*. Austin: University of Texas Press.

Bakhtin, M. (1968). *Rabelais and His World*. Cambridge, MA: MIT Press.

Bane, Michael, and Mary Ellen Moore (1981). *Tampa, Yesterday, Today, and Tomorrow*. Tampa, FL: Mishler and King.

Barkin, Gareth, and Glenn Davis Stone (2000). Anthropology: Blurring the Lines and Moving the Camera: The Beginnings of Web-Based Scholarship in Anthropology. *Social Science Computer Review* 18(2): 125–131.

———. (2004). Field Notes as Web Site: Integrating Multimedia into Anthropological Documents. *Field Methods* 16(2): 203–214.

Bateson, Gregory, and Margaret Mead. (1942). *Balinese Character: A Photographic Analysis*. New York: New York Academy of Sciences.

Becoming Human. Available at http://www.becominghuman.org. Accessed February 28, 2009.

Behar, Ruth (2003 [1993]). *Translated Woman: Crossing the Border with Esperanza's Story*. Boston: Beacon Press.

Berger, Arthur Asa (2002). *Video Games: A Popular Culture Phenomenon*. Edison, NJ: Transaction Publishers.

Bernard, H. Russell, and Michael J. Evans (1983). New Microcomputer Techniques for Anthropologists. *Human Organization* 42: 182–185.

Bigenho, Michelle (2002). *Sounding Indigenous: Authenticity in Bolivian Musical Performance*. New York: Palgrave Macmillan.

Billie Jean Isbell Andean Collection: Images from the Andes. Available at http://isbellandes.library.cornell.edu. Accessed February 28, 2009.

Bird, S. Elizabeth (2003). Imagining Indians: Negotiating Identity in a Media World. In S. Elizabeth Bird, ed., *The Audience in Everyday Life: Living in a Media World*. New York: Routledge. 86–117.

Boellstorff, Tom (2008). *Coming of Age in Second Life: An Anthropologist Explores the Virtually Human*. Princeton, NJ: Princeton University Press.

Boggs, Ralph Steele (1938). Spanish Folklore from Tampa, Florida. *Southern Folklore Quarterly* 2: 87–106.

———. (1937). Ybor City, Florida. *South Atlantic Bulletin* 3(2): 1–8.

Bolter, Jay David (2001). *Writing Space: Computers, Hypertext, and the Remediation of Print*. London: Taylor & Francis.

Bolter, Jay David, and Richard Grusin (2000). *Remediation: Understanding New Media*. Cambridge, MA: MIT Press.

Bowen, Elenore Smith [pen name of Laura Bohannan] (1964). *Return to Laughter: An Anthropological Novel*. New York: Anchor.

Brent, Edward E. Jr., and Ronald E. Anderson (1990). *Computer Applications in the Social Sciences*. Philadelphia: Temple University Press.

Brown, Karen McCarthy (2001). *Mama Lola: A Vodou Priestess in Brooklyn*. Berkeley: University of California Press.

Brown, Michael F. (2003). Weaving a Book into the Web. *Anthropology News* 44(8): 21.

Brynan, Lindsay (1939). A Study of the Latin Press in Ybor City, Tampa, Florida. *Works Progress Administration*: 1–16.

Calandra, Brendan, and John Lee (2005). The Digital History and Pedagogy Project: Creating an Interpretive/Pedagogical Historical Website. *The Internet and Higher Education* 8(4): 323–333.

Cameron, Fiona, and Helena Robinson (2007). Digital Knowledgescapes: Cultural, Theoretical, Practical, and Usage Issues Facing Museum Collection Databases in a Digital Epoch. In Fiona Cameron and Sarah Kenderdine, eds., *Theorizing Digital Cultural Heritage: A Critical Discourse*. Cambridge, MA: MIT Press. 165–192.

Cánepa, Gisela. (2001). *Identidades representadas: Performance, experiencia, y memoria en los Andes*. Lima: Pontificia Universidad Católica del Perú.

Canessa, Andrew (2000). Fear and Loathing on the Kharisi Trail: Alterity and Identity in the Andes. *The Journal of the Royal Anthropological Institute* 6(4): 705–720.

Center for Digital Storytelling. Available at http://www.storycenter.org. Accessed February 28, 2009.

Certeau, Michel de (1994). *La prise de parole et autres écrits politiques*. Paris: Sevil.

Champion, E. (2002). Cultural Engagement in Virtual Heritage Environments with Inbuilt Interactive Evaluation Mechanisms. Fifth Annual International Workshop, PRESENCE, Porto, Portugal.

Chase, Arlen F., Diane Z. Chase, and John F. Wieshampel (2010). Lasers in the Jungle: Airborne Sensors Reveal a Vast Maya Landscape. *Archaeology* 63(4): 27–29.

ChinaVine. Available at http://www.chinavine.org. Accessed February 28, 2009.

Christensen, Neil Blair (2003). *Inuit in Cyberspace: Embedding Offline, Identities Online*. Copenhagen: Museum Tusculanum Press.

Clifford, James, and George E. Marcus, eds. (1986). *Writing Culture: The Poetics and Politics of Ethnography*. Berkeley: University of California Press.

Congdon, Kristin G. (2002). *Uncle Monday and Other Florida Tales*. Jackson: University Press of Mississippi.

Consalvo, Mia (2003). Hot Dates and Fairy-Tale Romances: Studying Sexuality in Video Games. In Mark J. P. Wolf and Bernard Perron, eds., *The Video Game Theory Reader*. New York: Routledge. 275–302.

Coover, Roderick (2003). *Cultures in Webs* (CD-ROM). Watertown, MA: Eastgate Systems.

Crane, Gregory, Kalina Bontcheva, Jeffrey A. Rydberg-Cox, and Clifford Wulfman (2005). Emerging Language Technologies and the Rediscovery of the Past: A Research Agenda. *International Journal on Digital Libraries* 5(4): 309–316.

Cyber Anthropology. Available at http://www.carleton.ca/~bgiven /cyberant.htm. Accessed February 28, 2009.

CyberAnthropology Page. Available at www.fiu.edu/~mizrachs/cyber anthropos.html. Accessed February 28, 2009.

Damian, Carol Steve, S. Stein, and Nicario Jiménez Quispe (2004). *Popular Art and Social Change in the Retablos of Nicario Jiménez Quispe*. Lewiston, NY: Edwin Mellen Press.

De La Cadena, Marisol (2000). *Indigenous Mestizos: The Politics of Race and Culture in Cuzco, Peru, 1919–1991*. Durham, NC: Duke University Press.

Digital Ethnography Project. Available at (www.csus.edu/anth/research DigitalEthnographyProject.html). Accessed April 12, 2012.

Digital Himalaya. Available at http://www.digitalhimalaya.com. Accessed February 28, 2009.

Digital Humanities Exchange. Available at http://www.digitalhumanities.cah.ucf.edu/index.php. Accessed February 28, 2009 (not available as of April 12, 2012).

Duany, Jorge (2009). The Recent Puerto Rican Diaspora to Central Florida. Talk given at the exhibition opening of "Puerto Ricans in Central Florida 1940s–1980s: A History," Kissimmee, FL.

———. (2000). Nation on the Move: The Construction of Cultural Identities in Puerto Rico and the Diaspora. *American Ethnologist* 27(1): 5–30.

———. (1996). Review: Imagining the Puerto Rican Nation: Recent Works on Cultural Identity. *Latin American Research Review* 31(3): 248–267.

Dunn, Hampton (1972). *Yesterday's Tampa*. Miami, FL: E. A. Seemann Publishing.

East Mims Oral History Project Website. Available at pegasus.cc.ucf.edu/~cha/mims/welcometomims.html. Accessed February 28, 2009.

Escobar, Arturo (1994). Welcome to Cyberia: Notes on the Anthropology of Cyberculture. *Current Anthropology* 35(3): 211–231.

Experience Rich Anthropology. Available at http://lucy/ukc.ac.uk/HEFCE. Accessed February 28, 2009.

Fair, Rhonda S. (2000). Becoming the White Man's Indian: An Examination of Native American Tribal Web Sites. *The Plains Anthropologist* 45(172): 203–213.

Femenías, Blenda. (2005). *Gender and the Boundaries of Dress in Contemporary Peru*. Austin: University of Texas Press.

Fischer, Michael (1999). Worlding Cyberspace: Towards an Ethnography in Time, Space, and Theory. In George E. Marcus, ed., *Critical Anthropology Now: Unexpected Contexts, Shifting Constituencies, Changing Agendas*. Santa Fe, NM: School for American Research. 245–304.

Flores, Juan (2000). *From Bomba to Hip Hop: Puerto Rican Culture and Latino Identity*. New York: Columbia University Press.

Flynn, Bernadette. (2007). The Morphology of Space in Virtual Heritage. In Fiona Cameron and Sarah Kenderdine, eds., *Theorizing Digital Cultural Heritage: A Critical Discourse*. Cambridge, MA: MIT Press. 349–368.

Folkvine.org. Available at http://www.folkvine.org. Accessed February 28, 2009.

Forte, Maximilian (2004). Co-Construction and Field Creation: Website Development as Both Instrument and Relationship in Action Research. In Elizabeth A. Buchanan, ed., *Readings in Virtual Research Ethics: Issues and Controversies*. Hershey, PA: Information Science Publishing. 219–245.

Fuller, Mary, and Henry Jenkins (1995). Nintendo and the New World Travel Writing: A Dialogue. In Steve Jones, ed., *Cybersociety: Computer-Mediated Communication and Community*. Thousand Oaks, CA: Sage. 57–72.

García Canclini, Néstor (1995). *Hybrid Cultures: Strategies for Entering and Leaving Modernity*. Minneapolis: University of Minnesota Press.

Geertz, Clifford (1988). *Works and Lives: The Anthropologist as Author*. Palo Alto, CA: Stanford University Press.

———. (1973). *The Interpretation of Cultures: Selected Essays*. New York. Basic Books.

Gelleri, Gabor (2001). What Has to Do the Cyber with Anthropology and Anthropology with the Cyber? *Tabula* 4(2): 270–286.

Georges, Robert A., and Michael Owen Jones (1995). *Folkloristics: An Introduction*. Bloomington: Indiana University Press.

Giaccardi, Elissa, and Leysia Palen (2008). The Social Production of Heritage through Cross-Media Interaction: Making Place for Place-Making. *International Journal of Heritage Studies*, 14(3): 281–297.

Glassberg, David (1996). Public History and the Study of Memory. *The Public Historian* 18(2): 7–23.

Heider, Karl G. (2006). *Ethnographic Film*. 2nd ed. Austin: University of Texas Press.

Hesse-Biber, Sharlene, Paul R. DuPuis, and Kinder, T. Scott (1997). Anthropology: New Developments in Video Ethnography and Visual Sociology—Analyzing Multimedia Data Qualitatively. *Social Science Computer Review* 15(1): 5–12.

Hine, Christine (2000). *Virtual Ethnography*. London: Sage.

Hockey, Susan (2006). The Rendering of Humanities Information in a Digital Context: Current Trends and Future Developments. *Aslib Proceedings* 58(1/2): 89–101.

Howard, Robert Glenn (2008). Electronic Hybridity: The Persistent Processes of the Vernacular Web. *Journal of American Folklore* 121 (480): 192–218.

Hurston, Zora Neale (1998 [1937]). *Their Eyes Were Watching God*. New York: Harper Perennial.

Hypermedia Ethnography. Available at http://www.cf.au.uk/socsi/hyper .index.html. Accessed February 28, 2009.

Ingalls, Robert P., and Louis A. Perez Jr. (2003). *Tampa Cigar Workers: A Pictorial History*. Gainesville: University Press of Florida.

iNtergraph: Journal of Dialogic Anthropology. Available at http://inter graph-journal.com/enhanced/welcome2.htm). Accessed February 28, 2009 (not available as of April 12, 2012).

Isbell, Billie Jean (2009). *Finding Cholita*. Champaign: University of Illinois Press.

Jenkins, Henry (2004). Game Design as Narrative Architecture. In

Noah Wardrip-Fruin and Pat Harrington, eds., *First Person: New Media as Story, Performance, and Game*. Cambridge, MA: MIT Press. 118–130.

Jenkins, Henry, and David Thorburn, eds. (2004). *Democracy and New Media*. Cambridge, MA: MIT Press.

Karaganis, Joe (2007). *Structures of Participation in Digital Culture*. New York: Social Science Research Council.

Kenderdine, Sarah (2007). Speaking in Rama: Panoramic Vision in Cultural Heritage Visualization. In Fiona Cameron and Sarah Kenderdine, eds., *Theorizing Digital Cultural Heritage: A Critical Discourse*. Cambridge, MA: MIT Press. 301–332.

Koster, Ralph (2004). *A Theory of Fun for Game Design*. Phoenix, AZ: Paraglyph Press.

La Farge, Oliver (2004 [1929]). *Laughing Boy: A Navajo Love Story*. Boston: Mariner Books.

Landow, George P. (2006). *Hypertext 3.0: Critical Theory and New Media in an Era of Globalization*. Baltimore, MD: Johns Hopkins University Press.

Lanham, Richard A. (1995). *The Electronic Word: Democracy, Technology, and the Arts*. Chicago: University of Chicago Press.

La Rosa, Michael J., and Germán R. Mejía (2006). *An Atlas and Survey of Latin American History*. Armonk, NY: M.E. Sharpe.

Leonard, David J. (2006). Not a Hater, Just Keepin' It Real: The Importance of Race- and Gender-Based Game Studies. *Games and Culture* 1(1): 83–88.

Lévi-Strauss, Claude (1969). *The Raw and the Cooked*. New York: Harper and Row.

Lusenet, Yola de (2007). Tending the Gardens or Harvesting the Fields: Digital Preservation and the UNESCO Charter on the Preservation of the Digital Heritage. *Library Trends* 56(1): 164–182.

Lüthi, Max (1976). *Once Upon a Time: On the Nature of Fairy Tales*. Bloomington: Indiana University Press.

Marion, Jonathan S., and Julia Lynn Offen (2009). Translating Multisensory Experience: An Introduction. *Anthropology News* 50(4): 13–14.

McDaniel, Rudy, and Natalie Underberg (2007). Exembellishment: Using the eXtensible Markup Language as a Tool for Storytelling Research. *International Digital Media Arts Journal* 4(2): 56–69.

McGregor, Georgia (2007). Situations of Play: Patterns of Spatial Use in Videogames. DiGRA 2007 Conference, Tokyo, Japan.

Mead, Margaret (1930). *Coming of Age in Samoa: A Psychological Study of Primitive Youth for Western Civilization*. New York: William Morrow.

Mendoza, Zoila S. (2000). *Shaping Society through Dance: Mestizo Ritual*

Performance in the Peruvian Andes. Chicago: University of Chicago Press.

Messerli, Alfred (2005). Spatial Representation in European Popular Fairy Tales. *Marvels and Tales* 19(2): 274–284.

Miller, Daniel, and Don Slater (2001). *The Internet: An Ethnographic Approach*. Oxford: Berg.

Mitchell, Richard G. Jr., and Kathy Charmaz. (1998). Telling Tales and Writing Stories: Postmodernist Visions and Realist Images in Ethnographic Writing. In Scott Grills, ed., *Doing Ethnographic Research: Fieldwork Settings*. Thousand Oaks, CA: Sage. 228–248.

Moličnik, Vesna (1999). A Guide for Internet Sources in Anthropology, Ethnography, Ethnology and Folklore Studies. *Glasnik slovenskega etnoloskega Drustva* 39(2): 43–47.

Moore, Patrick, and Kate Hennessey (2006). New Technologies and Contested Ideologies: The Tagish FirstVoices Project. *The American Indian Quarterly* 30(1–2): 119–137.

Mormino, Gary R., and Anthony P. Pizzo (1983). *Tampa: The Treasure City*. Tulsa, OK: Continental Heritage Press.

Morris, Sue (2004). Co-Creative Media: Online Multiplayer Computer Game Culture. *SCAN: Journal of Media Arts Culture 1* (1). Available at http://scan.net.au/scan/display.php.?journal_id=16. Accessed April 12, 2012.

Murfin, Ross C., and Surpryia M. Ray (1997). *The Bedford Glossary of Critical and Literary Terms*. Boston: Bedford/St. Martin's.

Murray, Janet (1997). *Hamlet on the Holodeck: The Future of Narrative in Cyberspace*. New York: Free Press.

Myerhoff, Barbara (1980). *Number Our Days: A Triumph of Continuity and Culture among Jewish Old People in an Urban Ghetto*. New York: Touchstone.

Narayan, Kirin (1999). Ethnography and Fiction: Where Is the Border? *Anthropology and Humanism* 24(2): 134–147.

Paccagnella, Luciano (1997). Getting the Seat of Your Pants Dirty: Strategies for Ethnographic Research on Virtual Communities. *Journal of Computer Mediated Communication* 3(1): 267–288.

Pack, Sam (2006). How They See Me vs. How I See Them: The Ethnographic Self and the Personal Self. *Anthropological Quarterly* 79(1): 105–122.

Packer, Randall, and Ken Jordan (2002). *Multimedia: From Wagner to Virtual Reality*. New York: W. W. Norton.

Pearce, Jamie, Karen Witten, and Phil Bartie. (2006). Neighbourhoods and Health: A GIS Approach to Measuring Community Resource Accessibility. *Journal of Epidemiology and Community Health* 60: 389–395.

Peers, Laura, and Alison K. Brown (2003). *Museums and Source Communities: A Routledge Reader*. New York: Routledge.

PeruDigital. Available at http://www.perudigital.org. Accessed February 28, 2009.

Pfaffenberger, Brian (1990). *Democratizing Information: Online Databases and the Rise of End-User Searching*. Boston: G.K. Hall.

Pink, Sarah (2003). Representing the Sensory Home. Ethnographic Experience and Anthropological Hypermedia. *Social Analysis* 47(3): 46–63.

———. (2001). *Doing Visual Ethnography: Images, Media and Representation in Research*. London: Sage.

Podolevsky, Aaron (1987). New Tools for Old Jobs: Computers in the Analysis of Fieldnotes. *Anthropology Today* 3(5): 14–16.

Podolevsky, Aaron, and Christopher McCarty (1983). Topical Sorting: A Technique for Computer Assisted Qualitative Data Analysis. *American Anthropologist* 85(4): 886–890.

Porter, Noah (2004). CMA Introduction, Part 2: A Brief History of Computer-Mediated Anthropology. Available at http://www.anthropology.usf.edu/cma/cmahistory.htm. Accessed February 28, 2009.

RACE: Are We So Different? Available at http://www.understandingrace.org/HOME.HTML.

Ray, Shari (2004). *Gender Inclusive Game Design: Expanding the Market*. Hingham, MA: Charles River Media.

Redding, Terry, ed. (1999). Applied Anthropology on the Internet: Communication and Innovation. Available at http://www.aaa.net.org/napa/publications/napa19/onetheory.html. Accessed February 28, 2009.

Romero, Raúl (2001). *Debating the Past: Music, Memory, and Identity in the Andes*. New York: Oxford University Press.

———. (1993). *Música, danzas, y máscaras en los Andes*. Lima: Instituto Riva Agüero.

Ruby, Jay (1996). Visual Anthropology. In David Levinson and Melvin Ember, eds., *Encyclopedia of Cultural Anthropology*. Vol. 4. New York: Henry Holt. 1345–1351.

———. (1980). Exposing Yourself: Reflexivity, Anthropology, and Film. *Semiotica* 30 (1/2): 153–179.

Schuler, Douglas, and Aki Namioka, eds. (1993). *Participatory Design: Design Principles and Practices*. Oxford: Routledge.

Schwimmer, Brian (1997). *Hypertext Structures and Ethnographic Comparison as Implemented in "Kinship and Social Organisation: An Interactive Tutorial."* Available at http://www.umanitoba.ca/faculties/arts//anthropology/tutor/aaa_presentation.html. Accessed: April 12, 2012.

———. (1996). Anthropology on the Internet: A Review and Evaluation of Networked Resources. *Current Anthropology* 37(3): 561–568.

Silver, David (2000). Looking Backwards, Looking Forward: Cyberculture Studies 1990–2000. In David Gauntlett, ed., *Web.studies: Rewiring Media Studies for the Digital Age*. Oxford: Oxford University Press: 19–30.

Society for Visual Anthropology. Available at http://societyforvisual anthropology.org. Accessed February 28, 2009.

Solomon, Scott (2009). Lucy 2.0: Famous Fossil Hominid Goes Digital. Available at http://www.wired.com/wiredscience/2009/02/lucy/. Accessed February 28, 2009.

Sproull, Lee S., and Robert F. Sproull (1982). Managing and Analyzing Behavioral Records: Explorations in Nonnumeric Data Analysis. *Human Organization* 41(4): 283–290.

Squire, Kurt (in press). Civilization III as a World History Sandbox. In M. Bittanti, ed., *Civilization and Its Discontents. Virtual History: Real Fantasies*. Milan, Italy: Ludilogica Press.

Stahl, Sandra Dolby (1983). *Literary Folkloristics and the Personal Narrative*. Bloomington: Indiana University Press.

Stone, Glenn Davis (1998). Anthropology: Implications for Form and Content of Web-Based Scholarship. *Social Science Computer Review* 16: 4–15.

Taylor, T. L. (2006). *Play Between Worlds: Exploring Online Game Culture*. Cambridge, MA: MIT Press.

Taylor, T. L., and Beth Kolko (2003). Boundary Spaces: Majestic and the Uncertain Status of Knowledge. *Information, Communication and Society* 6(4): 497–522.

Tews, Rebecca R. (2001). Archetypes on Acid: Video Games and Culture. In Mark J. Wolf, ed., *The Medium of the Video Game*. Austin: University of Texas Press. 169–182.

Titon, Jeff Todd (1995). Text. *Journal of American Folklore* 108: 432–448.

TurboSquid. Available at http://www.turbosquid.com. Accessed February 28, 2009.

Turino, Thomas (1993). *Moving Away from Silence: Music of the Peruvian Altiplano and the Experience of Urban Migration*. Chicago: University of Chicago Press.

Ulfe, María Eugenia (2009). Representaciones del (y lo) indígena en los retablos peruanos. *Boletín del Instituto Francés de Estudios Andinos* 38(2): 307–326.

———. (2005). *Representations of Memory in Peruvian Retablos*. Doctoral dissertation, George Washington University, Washington, DC.

———. (2004). El arte de los retablos ayacuchanos: Religiosidad, historia y práctica cultural emergente. In Angeli Nori, ed., *Prácticas evangelizadoras, representaciones artísticas y contrucción del catolicismo en América, siglos XVII–XX*. Lima: Pontificia Universidad Católica del Perú. 73–99.

Underberg, Natalie M. (2010). Negotiating Puerto Rican Identity in Central Florida and Online. *Centro Journal* 22(1): 117–127.

———. (2008). The Turkey Maiden Educational Computer Game. *Folklore* 119(2): 201–217.

———. (2006a). *Ethnographic Storytelling on the Internet: Folkvine.org and the East Mims Oral History Project Website.* Paris: Ethnographic Film Panorama.

———. (2006b). Virtual and Reciprocal Ethnography on the Internet: The East Mims Oral History Project Web Site. *Journal of American Folklore* 119(473): 301–311.

———. (2001). Sor Juana's Villancicos: Context, Gender and Genre. *Western Folklore* 60(4): 297–316.

UNESCO (2001). Symposium on Indigenous Identities: Oral, Written Expressions and New Technologies. Available at Portal.unesco.org /culture/en/files/36904/12075601861/Symposium.pdf. Accessed February 28, 2009.

Van Maanen, John (1988). *Tales of the Field: On Writing Ethnography.* Chicago: University of Chicago Press.

Varese, Stefano (2006) *Witness to Sovereignty: Essays on the Indian Movement in Latin America.* Copenhagen: International Work Group for Indigenous Affairs.

Watkins, Jerry (2007). Social Media, Participatory Design and Cultural Engagement. In Bruce Thomas, ed., *Proceedings of the 2007 Australasian Conference on Computer-Human Interaction Conference,* OZCHI 2007, Adelaide, Australia. 161–166.

Wesch, Michael. Digital Ethnography. Available at http://www.mediated cultures.net. Accessed February 28, 2009.

White, Douglas, and Gregory F. Truex (1998). Anthropology and Computing: The Challenges of the 1990s. *Social Science Computer Review* 6(4): 481–497.

Whitehead, Neil L., and Michael Wesch. (2009). Human No More: Digital Subjectivities in a Post-Human Anthropology. *Anthropology News* 50(9): 12.

Wresch, William (1996). *Disconnected: Haves and Have-Nots in the Information Age.* Piscataway, NJ: Rutgers University Press.

Wynn, Eleanor (1991). Taking Practice Seriously. In Joan Greenbaum and Morten Kyng, eds., *Design at Work: Cooperative Design of Computer Systems.* Hillsdale, NJ: Erlbaum. 45–64.

Zeitlyn, David (1998). Anthropology Nine Hundred Years after the Invention of Hypertext. Available at: http://www.sosig.ac.uk/iriss /papers/proceed.html. Accessed February 28, 2009 (not available as of April 12, 2012).

Zeitlyn, David, and Gustaff Houtman (1996). Anthropology and Infor-

mation Technology. *Anthropology Today*. Available at http://lucy.ukc
.ac.uk/rai/AnthToday/Zhout.html. Accessed April 12, 2012.

Zorn, Elayne, and Natalie Underberg (2009). Multisensory Immersion
in Virtual Spaces: PeruVine/PeruDigital. *Anthropology News* 50(4):
18–19.

Index

Numbers in italics refer to images.

Abón, Patricia, 87
Adams, Jo Anne, 35
Andean culture, 29–33, 84. *See also* Folkvine project
Anderson, Ronald E., 43
anthropology: and computer science training, 6–7, 15, 42–43; narrative trend in, 12, 17, 37; reflexive trend in, 33, 37; themes in, 36. *See also* collaboration; digital ethnography; *and individual subfields*
Anthropology News, 7, 18
Apache, 57
archaeology: use of digital technology, 4–5
arpillera, 84, 85
Asociación Borinqueña, La, 59

Barkin, Gareth, 43–45
Bateson, Gregory, 17
Becoming Human website, 6
Benedictine nuns, 52–55, *53*
Billie Jean Isbell Andean Collection: Images from the Andes, 6

Bird, S. Elizabeth, 13
Boellstorff, Tom, 13, 67, 74
Boggs, Ralph Steele, 74
Bolter, Jay David, 11
Brent, Edward E., Jr., 43
broadcast media, 62
Bush, Vannevar, 50
Bustamante, Alicia, 31

Cameron, Fiona, 45–46, 59, 62, 68, 69
Caracol, Belize, 5
Cardiff University, 12
Carrasquillo, Lilly, 26–27
Center for Digital Storytelling, 7
Centre for Social Anthropology and Computing, 44
Certeau, Michel de, 70–71
Champion, E., 37
Charmaz, Kathy, 20, 21
ChinaVine project, 5
Christensen, Neil Blair, 28
Civilization (game), 71
Clifton Colored School, 22
codified space, 80–81
collaboration: between technical

experts and cultural experts, 7, 8–9, 15, 47, 50–51, 63; and collaborative methods of using new media, 17, 18, 33–34; and participatory design, 34, 47, 86; in research, 24, 29
complementary duality (Andean), 29–33
Computer Applications in the Social Sciences, 43
computer games: and characterization, 70; and cultural diversity, 56; design of, 10; and the humanities, 51, 69; intersection of, with culture, 74; and spatial storytelling, 16, 69–73, 80–81; and user-driven navigation, 71, 76. *See also* game design; Turkey Maiden Educational Computer Game
computers, 11; and anthropologic scholarship, 44–45; and data analysis, 12, 15, 42–44; and multivocality, 45–46
Congdon, Kristin, 75
constructivist paradigm, 46, 57
Crane, Gregory, 47, 50–51
cultural anthropology: narrative trend in, 12. *See also* ethnography
culture: characterization of, 10, 18; of the Internet, 13; intersection of, with technology, 4–6
Current Anthropology, 45
cyberculture studies, 42; critical, 23, 34
cyberethnography, 13
cyberspace ethnography, 66–67

Daily Work (Jiménez), 32
Democracy and New Media (Jenkins and Thorburn), 62
dialogic spaces, 13

digital cultural heritage studies, 12–13, 16, 45–47; and multivocality, 45; and tourism, 68, 75; and virtuality, 68–69, 77
digital design, 23–24
Digital Diaspora, 52, 59–65; stages of development, 63–65
digital divide, 88
digital ethnography: and activism, 88; defined, 10; and hypertext, 44–45; role of ethnographer in, 7–10; storytelling in, 18, 20–23, 69–73, 85; as tool for creative cultural representation, 4, 14, 85–86; as tool for heritage-based education, 4, 15–16, 68–69, 81, 86; as tool for research and data analysis, 4, 12, 15, 43–47, 86; and use of web tools, 43–47; and use of XML, 48–55; and user experience, 10; and virtuality, 67–69, 74, 77. *See also* collaboration; digital media; multimedia ethnography; *and individual projects*
Digital Ethnography Project, 12, 37
Digital Himalaya project, 6
Digital Humanities Exchange (DHE), 51, 55–58
digital media: and characteristics of electronic text, 11–12; and culture, 66–67; design of layout and navigation in, 10, 22; immersive and interactive qualities of, 10, 11, 12–13, 18–19, 21–22, 36; risks of using to express creativity, 23, 34; and self-representation, 26–27, 28; software in, 7–8; use of, by different subfields of anthropology, 4–6. *See also* computer

games; computers; digital
    ethnography; game design
document type definition
    (DTD), 51
Drupal, 63
Duany, Jorge, 26, 60

East Mims Oral History Project,
    20, 22
epistemic relativist paradigm,
    46, 62
Escobar, Arturo, 66
ethnography: as process and
    product, 10. *See also* digital
    ethnography; multimedia
    ethnography
Ethnography for the Digital Age,
    12
EverQuest, 71
exembellishment, 51
"Exembellishment: Using the
    eXtensible Markup Lan-
    guage as a Tool for Storytell-
    ing Research" (McDaniel and
    Underberg), 52
Experience Rich Anthropology
    project, 44
Explore Art, 57, 63
extensible markup language
    (XML), 12; and data searches,
    15, 48–49, 55; description of,
    48–49; in the Digital Diaspora
    project, 63, 64; and ethnogra-
    phy and narrative, 48–55; and
    the humanities, 48–49; and
    vocation narrative, 52–55

Facebook, 61
Fair, Rhonda, 13
Federal Writers' Project Works
    Progress Administration
    (WPA), 56, 58, 75
feely, 23
Fischer, Michael, 66–67

Flickr, 58, 87
Florida Everglades Project, 72
Florida Humanities Council, 29
Flynn, Bernadette, 71–72, 77
folklore, 4, 19, 26, 33, 37. *See also*
    individual projects
folklorists, 52
folktale: Quechua, 85; represen-
    tation of space in, 79–80
Folkvine project, 7, 20, 22; as
    integration of Andean culture
    with website design, 29–33;
    and Lilly Carrasquillo, 26–27
Forte, Maximilian, 24, 29
Fuller, Mary, 69, 76

game design, 7–8, 9, 36, 37–38, 55.
    See also computer games
Geertz, Clifford, 17
Giaccardi, Elissa, 35
Grand Theft Auto, 71, 72

hakpaks, 75
Hallman, Beth, 35
Heider, Karl, 86
Hennessey, Kate, 8, 25, 28
heritage studies, 36
Hine, Christine, 24
Hockey, Susan, 49
holonovel, 23
Houtman, Gustaff, 42, 43
Howard, Robert Glenn, 62
HTML. *See* hypertext markup
    language
human-computer interaction
    (HCI) studies, 8, 23–24
humanities computing, 49
Hurston, Zora Neale, 86
hypermedia, 11, 12, 21–22. *See also*
    digital media
Hypermedia Ethnography web-
    site, 12
HyperResearch, 43
hypertext, 44–45, 62

hypertext markup language (HTML), 48
hypertext studies, 11, 14, 23, 36, 50

immersion: as quality of digital media, 10, 12–13, 18–19, 22, 76; and virtuality, 68–69, 71
"Indigenous Identities: Oral, Written Expressions and New Technologies" (UNESCO), 24
indigenous people: rights of, 24–25; use of digital technology for self-representation, 25–26
Institute of Ethnomusicology, 2, 6; and the PeruDigital project, 33, 34, 40
interactivity: as quality of digital media, 10, 18–19, 21, 22
iNtergraph: Journal of Dialogic Anthropology, 12
Internet: access to, 5; culture of, 13; and identity creation, 60; and oral history research, 63. *See also* websites
Interpretation of Cultures, The (Geertz), 17
Inuit identity, 28

Jenkins, Henry, 62, 69, 76
Jiménez, Nicario, 11, 29–33
Jordan, Ken, 21

Kanter, John, 45
Kenderdine, Sarah, 68, 69, 77
Kim, Si-Jung "Jun," 35, 88
Kuehling, Susanne, 18

La Prensa, 50, 52, 59–65. *See also* Digital Diaspora
Law and Order, 70
Ledesma, Norma, *87*

Leonard, David, 56
Lima, Peru, 1–4. *See also* Folkvine project
linguistic anthropology, 4–5, 6
literary anthropology, 4, 11, 14, 17; definition and example of, 20–21
López Antay, Joaquín, 31
Lord of Agony Festival, 39–40. *See also* Peru: festivals and folklore of
Lucy, 5
Lusenet, Yola de, 57
Lüthi, Max, 79

Marion, Jonathan S., 28
Martí, José, 78–79. *See also* Turkey Maiden Educational Computer Game
McDaniel, Rudy, 86–87
McDonnell, Bridget, 18
McGregor, Georgia, 80–81
Mead, Margaret, 17
Messerli, Alfred, 79
metadata, 12, 46, 48, 49, 51, 58, 60
Methodological Issues in Qualitative Data Sharing and Archiving, 12
Migration (Jiménez), 32
Miller, Daniel, 13
Mitchell, Richard G., Jr., 20, 21
Mobile Folk, 88
Moore, Patrick, 8, 25, 28
multimedia: defining features of, 21–22
multimedia ethnography, 10, 11; and boundary crossing, 17
multisensory ethnography, 10, 18, 28
multivocality, 19, 45, 86. *See also* narrative
Murray, Janet, 11, 23
museums, 46, 68

Nancy Drew, 70
narrative: digital, 7, 18–19;
   ethnography as, 10; nonlinear,
   22; *normalform*, 52, 54, 55; and
   spatial storytelling, 16, 18–19,
   69–73; and techniques of digital ethnographic storytelling,
   20–23; as trend in cultural
   anthropology, 12, 17, 37; user-
   generated, 62–63; vocation,
   52–55; and website design, 37.
   See also digital ethnography
native anthropologists, 8
network culture, 15
NeverWinter Nights, 56, 75
new media. *See* digital media
new media ethnography. *See* digital ethnography
New York Blackouts, 63
Nintendo, 70
nonplayable character (NPC),
   78, 79
normalform, 52, 54, 55

Offen, Julia Lynn, 28
online action research, 8, 24
optical character recognition
   (OCR), 64

Paccagnella, Luciano, 24
Packer, Randall, 105
Palen, Leysia, 35
participatory culture, 46–47, 57
participatory design (PD), 8, 9,
   14, 24; and the PeruDigital
   project, 34–36
Perseus Project, 63
Peru, 53: festivals and folklore
   of, 33, 34, 36, 38–40. *See also*
   Folkvine project; PeruDigital
   project
PeruDigital project, 1–4, 7, 11,
   19; design and production
   of, 33–38; expansion of, 87;

images from, 2, 3, 34, 38, 39,
   41; as multisensory ethnography, 18; narrative approach of,
   37; and partnership building
   trips, 34–35, 36; team involved
   with, 35–36, 87; user experience in, 38–41
PHP, 58
physical (biological) anthropology, 4, 6
Pink, Sarah, 11, 86
Pishtaku (Jiménez), 32
polysemic knowledge model, 46
Pontifical Catholic University of
   Peru–Lima, 6, 33
Production of Hypermedia
   Ethnography, 12
Puerto Rican population, 59–60
Puerto Ricans in Central Florida,
   1940s–1980s: A History, 19,
   19, 61

Quechua, 29–33, 38

RACE: Are We So Different?
   website, 5
reciprocal technology, 26
Redmon, Maria, 75
retablos, 29–33. *See also* Folkvine
   project
Robinson, Helena, 45–46, 59, 62,
   68, 69

Schwimmer, Brian, 42, 44
Second Life, 13, 67
Second Vatican Council, 53
Semantic Web, 48
sensory ethnography, 11
SGML, 48
Silver, David, 23
Sipapu website, 45
Slater, Don, 13
social media, 46–47, 61, 62. *See
   also individual sites*

Southern Folklore Quarterly, 75
Sproull, Lee S., 43
Sproull, Robert F., 43
Stone, Glen Davis, 43–45
storytelling. *See* narrative

Tagish FirstVoices Project, 25–26
technology: intersection of, with
    culture, 4–6; social impact of,
    4, 18. *See also* computers; digi-
    tal ethnography; digital media
text encoding initiative (TEI), 49
Themescaping Virtual Collec-
    tions, 68
Theory in Anthropology web-
    site, 45
Thorburn, David, 62
3-D, 45, 46, 58, 68, 77, 84
tonderos, 2, 3
transmedia story creation, 9, 36
tripartite division of time and
    space (Andean), 29–33
Truex, Gregory F., 42
TurboSquid, 57
Turkey Maiden Educational
    Computer Game, 8, 16, 19,
    51–52, 56, 58; development
    of, 74–75; lesson outline of,
    77–79; plot in, 75–79; repre-
    sentation of space in, 79–81;
    user agency in, 76
"Turkey Maiden, The" ("La
    Pavera"), 75–76
Twitter, 61

Ulfe, María Eugenia, 30
Ultima Online, 71
*Uncle Monday and Other Florida
    Tales*, 75
Underberg, Natalie, 4; and the
    Digital Diaspora project, 59;
    and East Mims Oral History
    Project, 22; and exembellish-
    ment, 51; and Folkvine proj-

ect, 29; and PeruDigital proj-
    ect, 33, 34, *36*; and Turkey
    Maiden Educational Com-
    puter Game, 52, 74, 75; and
    University of Central Florida
    Cultural Heritage Alliance,
    19–20
University of Central Florida
    Cultural Heritage Alliance, 19
University of Central Florida
    Digital Ethnography Lab, 4,
    19, 33; website of, *5, 19*
Unreal (game engine), 72

Valley of the Shadows, 57, 63
vernacular web, 62
video games. *See* computer games
Virgin of Candelaria festival, 1,
    38. *See also* Peru: festivals and
    folklore of
Virtual Institute of Mambila
    Studies, 44
virtuality, 67–69, 73
Virtual Taller, 84
visual anthropology, 11, 14, 17,
    42, 43
Visual Anthropology, 28

Web 2.0, 60–63, 87
websites: design of, 10, 14; as part
    of collaborative research, 24;
    use of, in digital ethnography,
    43–47
"Welcome to Cyberia: Notes on
    the Anthropology of Cyber-
    culture" (Escobar), 66
Wesch, Michael, 7, 13
White, Douglas, 42
Whitehead, Neil, 7
Wikipedia, 87
Wilk, Richard, 45

XML. *See* extensible markup
    language

Ybor City, Florida, 16, 19, 56, 74–75, 77–79; as Cigar Capital of the World, 75. *See also* Turkey Maiden Educational Computer Game

YouTube, 61, 87

Zárate, Flora, 84, *87*

Zeitlyn, David, 42, 43, 44

Zorn, Elayne, 4; and Folkvine project, 29; and PeruDigital project, 33, 34, *36*

Lightning Source UK Ltd.
Milton Keynes UK
UKHW010725280521
384458UK00012B/473